ABUNDANCE OF GRACE

The History of the Archdiocese of Seattle

1850 - 2000

ORIGINAL RESEARCH BY PATRICIA O'CONNELL KILLEN
EDITED BY CHRISTINE M. TAYLOR

Publisher: Éditions du Signe • B.P. 94 • 67038 Strasbourg • France

Publishing Director: Christian Riehl

Design and layout: Sylvie Reiss

Director of publication: Dr. Claude-Bernard Costecalde

Editorial support: Mary Cabrini Durkin, OSU

ISBN: 2-7468-0250-3

Printed in Italy by Stige

My Dear Friends in Christ:

As we cross the threshold of the new millennium, we mark the first 150 years of the Catholic Church in the Archdiocese of Seattle. When I arrived in 1997, I spoke of the transformative power of hope. Between impossibility and possibility is the threshold of hope. The potential of history to transform our lives lies across that threshold. We celebrate this passage as a community of faith rooted in a strong commitment to serving our Lord. By reflecting on our past we may look to the future renewed and full of hope.

This sesquicentennial history will provide you with an opportunity to learn more about our rich and diverse heritage. It includes stories of courage, sacrifice, commitment, and deep faith. The bishops, clergy, men and women religious, and laity who have gone before us have left us a tremendous legacy; one that we can build upon as we continue our journey of faith. The multifaceted and multicultural experiences of the men and women in this archdiocese are truly inspiring and truly humbling. We are challenged to learn from these experiences and grow in love and faith as we share the Good News of the Gospel Message.

Understanding our past allows us to face the future as a people transformed. What legacy shall we leave? I pray that the Holy Spirit will guide us through the challenges that lie ahead, and open our hearts and minds to God's healing light.

May God's blessings be yours.

Sincerely yours in Christ,

+ Alex J. Brunett

Most Rev. Alexander J. Brunett
Archbishop of Seattle

ACKNOWLEDGEMENTS

This book would not have been possible without the work and support of numerous individuals and institutions. Indeed their contributions to the entire project from inception to realization are proof of a vibrant and multifaceted Church. A special thanks goes to the staff of the Archives of the Archdiocese of Seattle, namely, J. Norman Dizon, Assistant Archivist; Sara Nau, Records Analyst; and Jessica Pitre-Williams, Project Assistant. The work of historian and theologian Patricia O'Connell Killen was indispensable in providing original research, conceptualization, and framework.

Among individuals at the chancery of the archdiocese who shared their experiences, expertise, and resources are (in alphabetical order) Veronica Leasiolagi Barber, Director of Asian/Pacific American Affairs; Maria Esther Bazan Myrick, Director of Hispanic Affairs; the Very Rev. Paul Magnano, Vicar for Clergy; Sharon Pitre-Williams, Director of African-American/Black Catholic Affairs; and Ray Williams, Director of Native American Affairs.

Many in the archdiocesan community are recognized for providing invaluable insight, photographs, or other materials: Gudelia Alejo, Mary M. Anderson, David Buerge, Pat Cashman, Fred and Dorothy Cordova, Rev. James Eblen, Bethel Graham, Chermaine Hayes, Marguerite Main, Sr. Uma McLoughlin, O.S.F., Cleo Molina, Dr. Jeanette Rodriguez, Dorren Beard Simpkins, Sr. Laura Swan, O.S.B., Kathy Williams Spencer, and Rev. Michael OBrien.

Interviews conducted with the following persons offered thought-provoking and unique perspectives: Gudelia Alejo, Rev. Msgr. John Doogan, the Very Rev. Joseph Doogan, Charles Gill, Alicia Gonzalez-Capestany, Walter Hubbard, Sr. Ann Noth, O.S.B., Clayton Pitre, Sharon Pitre-Williams, Martin Plamondon II, Very Rev. Michael G. Ryan, Elizabeth Thomas, Rev. William Treacy, Sr. Lucy Wynkoop, O.S.B., and members of the Asian/Pacific-American Ministries Advisory Council. Oral histories were gathered from Vernon Lane and Alexander Solomon of the Lummi Indian Nation; Wayne Williams of the Tulalip Tribe; Ida Williams and Ivan and Agnes Willup of the Swinomish Tribe.

The vision of professional photographers Mike Penney and Dan Schlatter is apparent throughout this publication; we are grateful for the permission to use their work. We are grateful as well to Martin Plamondon II who provided original map illustrations.

Historical societies, religious communities, and other archival repositories which granted permission to reprint photographs are: the Jesuit Oregon Province Archives for a portrait of Peter DeSmet, S.J., (neg. 802.01); the Sisters of Providence Archives for photos of the Vancouver convent, the founding sisters, and Our Lady of Seven Dolors School, Tulalip; the Sisters of St. Joseph of Peace for a photo of their community; the Sisters of St. Dominic, Congregation of St. Thomas Aquinas, for a class photo at Sacred Heart School, Seattle; the Diocese of Victoria for a portrait of Modeste Demers; the Museum of History and Industry, PEMCO Webster and Stevens Collection, for photos of the Duwamish tideflats (83.10.7767 and 83.104435.2) and Seattle's Hooverville (83.10.4435.2); Oregon State Historical Society for a Map of the U.S., Territory of Oregon, 1838 (neg. 101398, map 84) and Map of Ecclesiastical Province of Oregon, ca. 1846 (neg. 101400); and Washington State Historical Society for a portrait of Simon Plamondon (neg. port/plo2) and of John McLoughlin (neg. port/mc14).

There were innumerable individuals, offices, and organizations who provided assistance, support, and resources to ensure the successful completion of this project. We are truly grateful for the gifts they shared and for their encouragement and collaboration.

Christine Taylor

Chancellor

November, 2000

TABLE OF CONTENTS

ORIGINS OF THE DIOCESE OF NESQUALLY

Francis Norbert Blanchet

Today's Archdiocese of Seattle came into existence on May 31, 1850, when Pope Pius IX created the district of Nesqually into a diocese and transferred Bishop Augustin Magloire Alexandre Blanchet to that See from the Diocese of Walla Walla. The action came in response to a request formulated by Archbishop Francis Norbert Blanchet (his brother) of Oregon City, Bishop Modeste Demers of Vancouver Island and Bishop A.M.A. Blanchet of Walla Walla during the first provincial council of Oregon City held in late February of 1849. The ecclesiastical solemnness and formality of that council and its actions were a testimony to the vision of the first institutional leaders of the Catholic Church in the Pacific Northwest.

At the same time, however, they belied the fragility of the institutional structures, personnel, and monetary resources of the Roman Catholic Church in the entire Pacific Northwest at that time and for years to come. For more than half of its first 150 years, the Church in the Pacific Northwest was a missionary church, dependent on the vision, commitment, and courage of the Catholic people who wanted to live their faith, and the clergy

Oregon Territory, 1838

and religious who sought to pass on the gift of faith by building religious institutions and serving the pastoral, social, and educational needs of the people in a geographically daunting, multi-ethnic and sparsely populated area.

Roman Catholic priests arrived to stay in the Pacific Northwest only eleven years before the first provincial council of Oregon City. Fathers F.N. Blanchet and Demers traveled to Fort Vancouver with an annual Hudson's Bay Company provisioning brigade in 1838. They left St. Boniface, Manitoba, on July 10 and arrived at Fort Vancouver on November 24. The priests were sent by Bishop Joseph Signay of Quebec and his Auxiliary Bishop Joseph Provencher in the Red River country of present day Manitoba who, as Apostolic Vicar for the District of the Northwest, had responsibility for what is now the Pacific Northwest.

The priests undertook their journey in response to persistent requests from *Canadien* traders and *voyageurs* who had worked for various fur companies in what became the Columbia District of the Hudson's Bay Company during the 1820s and 1830s. Men such as Etienne Lucier, Joseph Gervais, Louis Labonte, Simon Plamondon and others wanted Catholic teaching and sacraments for their wives, mostly Native American, and their children. They also wanted to make sure that they would have the comfort of the church in their old age. Beginning in 1834, they wrote letters to Bishop Provencher requesting priests. These Canadian Catholic fur trade employees

INTERVIEW WITH

MARTIN PLAMONDON II

Simon Plamondon

"I am a ninth generation descendant of Philippe and Marguerite Plamondon of Montreal, Canada, part of the second wave of settlement to Western Washington that began with my grandfather, Isidore Plamondon. The first wave was begun by Simon Plamondon. In his teens, Simon and one of his brothers traveled from Montreal along the Great Lakes, south on the Mississippi to visit family in the Louisiana Territory. They then walked or canoed out the Missouri and over the mountains to the Pacific Coast where they worked at Fort George, Astoria, a small fur trading post. The brother apparently returned to Montreal and Simon moved to the newly established Fort Vancouver, 106 miles up the Columbia River, to work for Chief Factor John McLoughlin. Simon was a carpenter and also drove freight to the northern Hudson's Bay facilities on Puget Sound. Simon, not getting on with McLoughlin, took up residence at Plamondon (Cowlitz) Landing near present day Toledo, Washington. He was married to a Cowlitz Indian woman, the first of four Cowlitz wives according to the Tribe. Simon was the first non-Indian settler to live outside a fort in the present day state of Washington. Simon was a fifth generation descendant of Philippe. Simon's father, J. Baptiste, was a brother to my ancestor, Louis Plamondon."

John McLoughlin, Chief Factor of Hudson's Bay Company, Fort Vancouver

had maintained a sense of their Catholic identity while in the Company's service by securing a separate cemetery at the Hudson's Bay Company's Fort Vancouver. One testimony to their desire for priests is the story that Simon Plamondon, first white settler on the Cowlitz, on his way back from a trip to the Arctic, detoured to Quebec to carry the settlers' request for priests prior to returning to the Cowlitz in the spring of 1838.

Detail of Catholic ladder

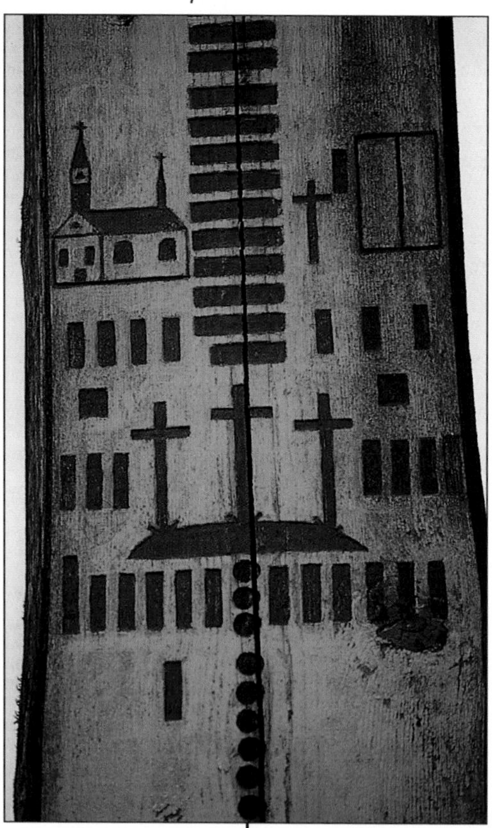

teaching. They focused on conveying in simple fashion the truths of the Catholic faith and bringing Native Americans to baptism.

Blanchet's and Demers' use of the Catholic Ladder, a pictorial representation of salvation history, became a focus in their contest with Protestant missionaries, such as the Methodists and those sponsored by the American Board of Commissioners for Foreign Missions (ABCFM). But the Catholic Ladder was not simply a tool in the battle between Catholic and Protestant evangelization efforts. It also facilitated Native American evangelization among Native Americans—one of the ways Catholicism had spread prior to the arrival of the two priests in the Columbia District, and would continue to spread throughout the entire Pacific Northwest.

Blanchet and Demers were sent to evangelize the Native Americans as well as to care for the Catholic employees and former employees of the Hudson's Bay Company. They preached missions to Catholics, Indians, and anyone else who would listen at the Hudson's Bay Company forts of Vancouver, Nisqually, Walla Walla, and Colville, the Company's Puget Sound Agricultural Company at Cowlitz Prairie, and at settlements in the Willamette Valley.

During the first part of the nineteenth century missions were a popular strategy of evangelization and pastoral practice. Missions went on for weeks at a time with talks, catechism instruction, and liturgy spread throughout the days and evenings. The sermons aimed to make people aware of the perils of sin, to animate their devotion to God, and to bring them back to the sacraments, especially confession, and the observance of the Church's moral teachings. Efforts to evangelize the Native Americans involved both missions and

Demers and Blanchet traveled extensively in present-day Oregon, Washington, Idaho, British Columbia, and Alberta, always following the Hudson's Bay Company routes. Church life followed economic life. The Company's system of forts and trade routes provided the only stable Euro-American infrastructure in the region during this period. Economic self-interest dictated avoiding the worst kinds of exploitation of Native Americans and destruction of their cultures. The Company's control of the region and relationship with Native Americans would be disrupted when the demand for furs dropped and the influx of settlers began in the 1840s.

By 1841 Demers and Blanchet became aware of the presence of Jesuits in the eastern portion of their mission. The Jesuits, headed by Father Peter DeSmet, went to the Flatheads, Nez Percé, and Coeur d'Alenes, and others, ostensibly at the request of Flatheads who had traveled to St. Louis seeking "blackrobes." While the French priests from Canada and the Jesuits from St. Louis worked to convert Indians, revive the faith of Catholics, and convert Euro-Americans who were not Catholic, both ecclesiastical and political events moved very quickly. The Columbia Mission, short-staffed and with limited resources, was carried out in a region that was jointly occupied by Great Britain and the United States.

The political settlement of joint occupancy, the desire of Bishop Signay of Quebec to be relieved of the burden of the Columbia Mission, and the desire of U.S. bishops to give the Rocky Mountain region and points further West to the Jesuits, all contributed to a sequence of events that would result in the creation of the ecclesiastical province of Oregon City in 1846, the second to be established in the United States.

On December 1, 1843, Pope Gregory XVI, issued a brief constituting "all the territory between the Mexican province of California on the south, and the Russian province of Alaska on the north," and extending "from the Pacific Ocean to the Rocky Mountains" into an apostolic vicariate with Francis Norbert Blanchet as bishop.

Less than a month after receiving the news, Blanchet left for Canada by boat and arrived in Quebec in late June. He was consecrated by Bishop Ignace Bourget on July 25, 1845 in St. James Cathedral, Montreal. A month later,

Peter DeSmet, S.J.

Blanchet sailed for Europe to seek funds and personnel for the new apostolic vicariate. He spent four months in Rome during which time he submitted to the Sacred Congregation of Propaganda his *Memoriale*, a proposal to erect the apostolic vicariate into an ecclesiastical province of Oregon City with seven suffragan bishops dependent on an archdiocese. Blanchet reasoned that this arrangement would allow the Catholic Church in Oregon Country to avoid the loss of souls that had attended California's separation from Mexico.

On July 24, 1846, Pius IX raised Blanchet's apostolic vicariate to the Ecclesiastical Province of Oregon City, with Blanchet elevated to Archbishop. Modeste Demers was appointed to the Diocese of Vancouver Island and Augustin Magloire Blanchet was appointed to the Diocese of Walla Walla. Five other districts were placed under the three dioceses: Nesqually, Fort Hall, Colville, Princess Charlotte, and New Caledonia. All this for an area that, by F.N. Blanchet's own reckoning, included only 6,000 Catholics, over 5,000 of whom were Native American. The erection of the Archdiocese of Oregon City and its suffragan sees occurred less than six weeks after formal settlement of joint occupancy of the Oregon Country in favor of the United States. The Oregon Treaty, signed June 10, 1846 established the boundary between the U.S. and Great Britain at the 49th parallel.

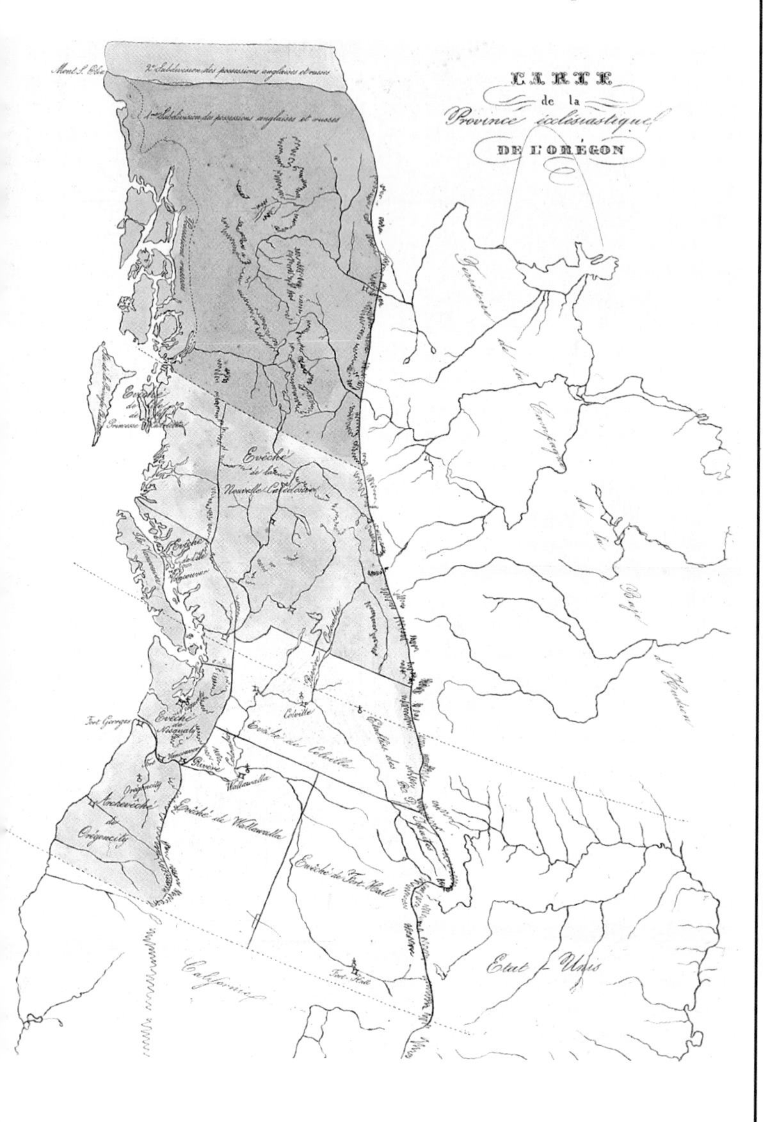

Ecclesiastical Province of Oregon, ca. 1846

A.M.A. Blanchet was consecrated Bishop of Walla Walla on September 27, 1846, by Bishop Ignace Bourget, in St. James Cathedral, Montreal. In the months between his consecration and his departure for the Oregon Country on March 23, 1847, Blanchet sought funds and personnel for the new diocese. Father Jean Baptiste Brouillet was released to serve as Vicar General. He also took with him two seminarians, William LeClaire and Louis P. Rousseau, and the promise that priests of the Order of the Oblates of Mary Immaculate would work in his diocese. (The Oblates who joined him at St. Louis, Missouri, were: P. Richard, superior; E.C. Chirouse and J.C. Pandosy, clerics; and George Blanchet, lay brother.)

Unlike his brother, A.M.A. Blanchet and his companions traveled to Oregon Country via the Oregon Trail. Blanchet's journal for this trip not only details the trials of travel by foot, wagon, and horseback across the continent, but also provides his impressions of people in the United States and the state of the Catholic Church here. He noted that American men could be identified by their practice of putting their feet up on tables, chairs, or other surfaces whenever they sat down. On the whole he found the Catholic Church in the United States less well off and its people less devout, less respectful of ecclesiastical authority, and less adept with liturgical ceremony than his French Canadian compatriots in Quebec.

By August 7, 1847, Blanchet's party had reached Fort Hall. Blanchet separated from the bulk of his party and the wagons and rode ahead with one companion. He arrived at Fort Walla Walla on September 5, 1847. This Hudson's Bay Company post was the See of the new Diocese. Before the end of the month he met Dr. Marcus Whitman whose ABCFM-sponsored Protestant mission, Waiilatpu, was nearby. Whitman was not pleased to have a Catholic presence in the region and made this clear to the bishop. On October 3, 1847 the remaining members of Blanchet's party arrived. The Oblates of Mary Immaculate soon left to establish St. Rose Mission on the Yakima River and Brouillet opened St. Anne Mission for the Cayuse (about 25 miles from the Whitman Mission) on November 27, 1847.

When Blanchet and his associates arrived at Walla Walla, the Cayuse were already suffering from a measles epidemic. The death of large numbers, especially children, aggravated the hostility toward Marcus Whitman that had been growing among this tribe for some time. When Whitman's medicine failed to heal the children a rumor began that he was poisoning the Indians in an effort to get their land. That rumor, coupled with the increasingly large number of immigrants from the United States who crossed Cayuse lands on the Oregon Trail, contributed to what became known as the Whitman Massacre. In the mid-afternoon of November 29, Dr. Marcus Whitman, his wife, Narcissa, Prentiss Whitman, and eight additional men at the mission were killed by one group of Cayuse. Forty-seven other men, women, and children were taken prisoner.

Brouillet heard about it on November 30; on December 1, he hastened to Waiilatpu. He helped bury the dead and sought assurances from the Indians for the safety of the captives. Two more captives, both men ill with the measles, were murdered after Brouillet left Waiilatpu to return to St. Anne's with hopes of

Excerpt from A.M.A. Blanchet's journal

PIUS PP. IX.

Appointment of A.M.A. Blanchet as Bishop of Walla Walla, 1846

JEAN BAPTISTE ABRAHAM BROUILLET

Jean Baptiste Abraham Brouillet was born on December 11, 1813 in Quebec, Canada. He was ordained for the Diocese of Montreal on August 27, 1837. In 1847, he was granted permission to become a missionary in the Northwest, and accompanied Bishop A.M.A. Blanchet to the new Diocese of Walla Walla.

Upon arrival at Fort Walla Walla in the spring of 1847, Brouillet opened St. Anne's mission among the Cayuse Indians, near the Umatilla River in what is now the southeastern border area of Washington.

Brouillet's involvement in the aftermath of the Whitman Massacre led to accusations that the Catholic missionaries and members of the Hudson's Bay Company were responsible for the tragedy.

Belief in the culpability of the Catholic Church in the massacre was so widespread that Brouillet wrote a pamphlet in 1848 in defense of his actions.

Brouillet was appointed vicar general of the Diocese of Nesqually and became known as a strong mediator and administrator. His pastoral work involved ministry to Native Americans and to French Canadians in the Pacific Northwest. His work as vicar general often sent him to Washington D.C. on business relating to Catholic Church land claims as well as the interests of Native Americans.

In 1874, Brouillet was released from the diocese to work on behalf of Catholic Native American missions throughout the country. He became director and treasurer of the Bureau of Catholic Indian Missions and worked with General Charles Ewing in administering the complex details of President Grant's peace policy. He died on February 5, 1884 in Washington D.C., and is buried at Mt. Olivet Cemetery.

intercepting the other Protestant missionary in the area, Rev. Henry Spalding who he knew was headed for Waiilatpu.

Brouillet succeeded in saving Spalding's life. In the weeks that followed Bishop Blanchet, Brouillet and Peter Skene Ogden of the Hudson's Bay Company were deeply involved in securing the release of the captives from Waiilatpu as well as from Spalding's Lapwai mission. On December 29, Ogden arrived at Fort Walla Walla with ransom goods and sixteen paddlers to secure the hostages. On that same day the Cayuse chiefs had gathered at the Catholic mission at Umatilla, and with Bishop Blanchet's assistance, prepared a petition to Governor Abernathy of the Oregon Provisional Government, asking for a peace conference and offering to give up the prisoners.

Ogden called a council of the Cayuse chiefs at Fort Walla Walla and asked the bishop to attend. The Indians agreed to turn over the captives. Hudson's Bay Company paid the ransom and the hostages from Waiilatpu were brought to Fort Walla Walla. The group waited for the hostages from Lapwai. Ogden and Blanchet were anxious to begin the trip to Fort Vancouver with the hostages as soon as possible, hoping to dampen the enthusiasm of American Willamette Valley volunteers who were reportedly assembling to attack the Cayuse.

Eugene Casimir Chirouse, O.M.I.

In this tense situation, Blanchet ordained to the priesthood the two Oblate candidates who had accompanied him to Walla Walla: Eugene Casimir Chirouse and Charles Pandosy. These were the first ordinations to the priesthood in present-day Washington State. Both men returned to the Oblate mission among the Yakimas and would spend their lives working with various Native American tribes throughout Washington State and in British Columbia.

Charles Pandosy, O.M.I.

Once the hostages were taken to Fort Vancouver, Blanchet traveled to St. Paul. This was the occasion for the first provincial Council of Oregon City, February 28 - March 1,

L-r: A.M.A. Blanchet, F.N. Blanchet, Modeste Demers

1848, during which time the bishops developed the request that Nesqually be established as a diocese and that A.M.A. Blanchet be transferred there. When Blanchet attempted to return to Walla Walla after the Council, the superintendent of Indian Affairs at The Dalles denied him passage.

At The Dalles, larger events that would affect Blanchet's current and future dioceses transpired rapidly. The Oregon Provisional Legislature considered and voted on a law that would have expelled all Catholic clergy from Oregon. The legislation emerged out of growing anti-Catholic sentiment fueled by Spalding's claim that Blanchet and Brouillet had encouraged the Waiilatpu killings, as well as the presumption that a load of guns and ammunition intended for the Indians at Jesuit missions in Montana and Idaho were meant to assist the Indians fighting in the Cayuse War.

On August 14, 1848, Congress established the territorial government of Oregon, which promised an end to the provisional government of Oregon and better protection for Catholics before the law. Also, 1848 witnessed the sinking of the *Vancouver* at the mouth of the Columbia. The *Vancouver* was bearing provisions for the Catholic missions of Oregon for the year—all supplies were lost. Distance and cost meant these supplies could not be easily replaced. The loss was aggravated as revolutions in Europe dried up the funds from the Society for the Propagation of the Faith on which Blanchet depended for supplies and support.

Then, in 1848 and 1849, the California Gold Rush drained the Euro-American population of the Oregon Country. The Willamette Valley and Vancouver area experienced severe population changes because of the mass exodus to the gold fields. Few made fortunes and many died of fever.

The Cayuse War ended in 1850, and territorial authorities demanded the extradition

PIUS PP. IX.

Decree establishing the Diocese of Nesqually, 1850

Augustin Magloire Alexandre Blanchet

of the Indians who murdered the Whitmans and others. The Cayuse chiefs responded that the ten Indians were dead, but the U.S. territorial officials continued to press the chiefs. To relieve their people, the chiefs found five men who consented to go down to Oregon City to meet with government officials and convince them the murderers were dead. They were arrested upon arrival and charged with murder. On May 27, 1850, all five were sentenced to hang. Archbishop F. N. Blanchet responded to the condemned men's request for a priest. After being baptized they were executed on June 3, 1850, in Oregon City.

Pope Pius IX, in a brief dated May 31, 1850, established the Diocese of Nesqually and named A.M.A. Blanchet the bishop. On October 27, 1850, Blanchet moved to Vancouver, Washington, the See city of the new diocese. No longer the seat of government or the center of civic and cultural life for the region as it had been ten years before, Vancouver was not a promising place. But A.M.A. Blanchet, a man of courage, faithfulness, and vision, took up residence in the frame house near St. James Cathedral and earnestly took up the task of organizing a diocese. Here he would build the Church, an institution that offered the gift of faith and the divine nourishment of the sacraments. In his journal for January 23, 1851, Blanchet wrote:

•

"The Blessed Sacrament is placed in the tabernacle for the first time since the foundation of the Mission at Vancouver. The tabernacle is lined only with white cotton while we wait to get some silk. The church, dedicated to St. James is then, at this moment truly, the House of God and the Gate of Heaven. We can say now; The Lord has sanctified this house which was built to establish His name here, and His eyes and His heart will always be there."

CHAPTER 1

ESTABLISHMENT OF THE DIOCESE OF NESQUALLY, 1850-1896

St. James Cathedral, Fort Vancouver

When A.M.A. Blanchet took up permanent residence at Vancouver, he found a small, unfinished church without ceiling or inside woodwork in which services had been held since 1846. The building was 36 x 70 feet in size. Named St. James, this was his cathedral church. Determined not to leave his diocese a legacy of debt, Blanchet refused to spend his scarce resources on a cathedral. His first priority was his pastoral mission.

Blanchet's cathedral symbolized the inauspicious circumstances under which he began his work as bishop of the Diocese of Nesqually. Until the time of his retirement in 1879, Blanchet faced a continuing series of seemingly endless challenges, among them insufficient finances and personnel, difficulties in communication and transportation, wars between Native American tribes and the federal government, shifting federal policies relating to Native Americans, anti-Catholic sentiment, and a highly mobile population.

That mobility was fueled by the California Gold Rush in 1848 and the subsequent gold, silver, lead and coal strikes in present-day Washington, Idaho, and British Columbia in the 1850s through the 1880s. The Oregon Donation Land Law of 1850, the Civil War of 1861-1865, and the Homestead Act of 1862 spurred increased migration to the territory. All of this altered the context within which Blanchet sought to build the Church. Despite the fluid and seemingly constantly changing context, the bishop's vision of the church and his commitment to his pastoral vocation gave him the courage to continue his work.

Fort Vancouver, 1855

During the nearly thirty years of Blanchet's episcopate, multiple factors contributed to the dramatic changes in the diocese. The geographic boundaries of the diocese were altered three times. The situation of Native Americans in the diocese deteriorated radically. The Euro-American population of the diocese increased markedly. And, with the assistance of money and personnel from Quebec, Europe, and Mexico, Blanchet succeeded in constructing institutions that were essential in providing effective pastoral and catechetical ministry for the people of the diocese.

When Blanchet was appointed Bishop of Nesqually, the districts of Colville and Fort Hall (eastern Washington, Idaho, western Montana) and the Diocese of Walla Walla (southeastern Washington, central, southern Idaho, southern Montana, northeastern Wyoming) were attached to the Archdiocese of Oregon City. In 1853, the district of Colville south of the 49th parallel, and those portions of the district of Fort Hall and the now suppressed Diocese of Walla Walla north of the 46th parallel, were attached to the Diocese of Nesqually. Blanchet's pastoral charge now included all the territory from the 46th parallel on the south, to the Canadian border to the north, to the Pacific Ocean in the west, to the Rocky Mountains in the east.

In 1868, the Apostolic Vicariate of Idaho, which included the current state of Idaho and western Montana, was created from the eastern portion of lands attached to the Diocese of Nesqually. From 1868 the borders of the diocese remained stable until the erection of the Diocese of Spokane in 1913 and the Diocese of Yakima in 1951.

Blanchet had come to the Oregon Country with dreams of re-establishing a French Catholic community of faith and culture that he perceived had been destroyed in France and was being dismantled in Lower Canada.

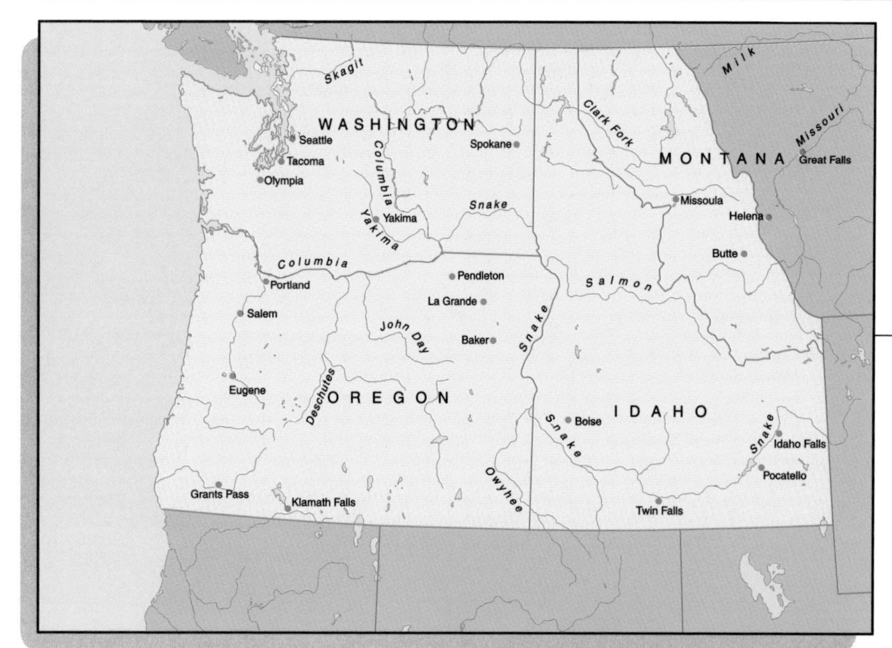

VICARIATE
OF OREGON CITY
1 8 4 6

DIOCESE
OF NESQUALLY
1 8 5 0 - 1 8 5 3

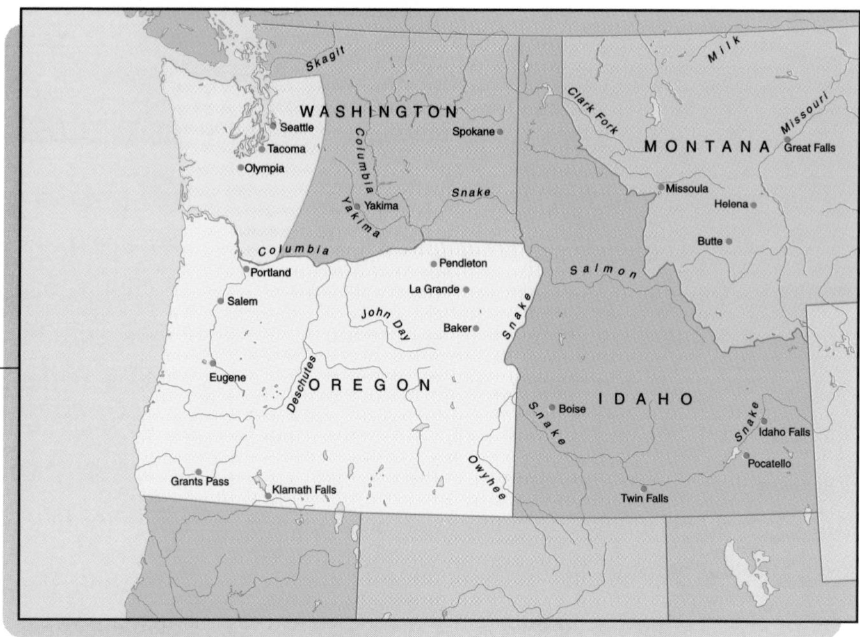

DIOCESE
OF NESQUALLY
1 8 5 3 - 1 8 6 8

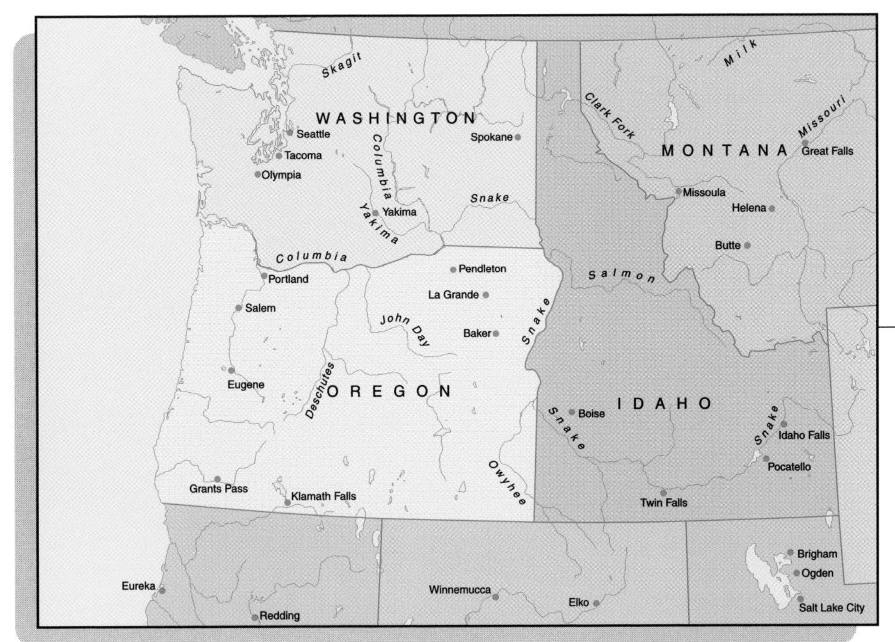

DIOCESE OF NESQUALLY*

1868 - 1913

*Name changed from Diocese of Nesqually to Diocese of Seattle in 1907

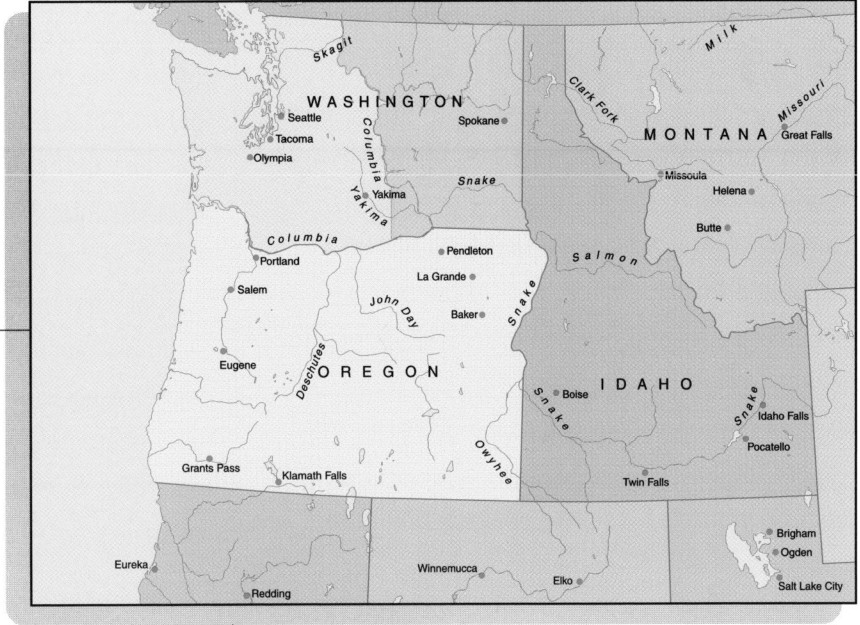

DIOCESE OF SEATTLE

1913 - 1951

ARCHDIOCESE OF SEATTLE

1951 - PRESENT

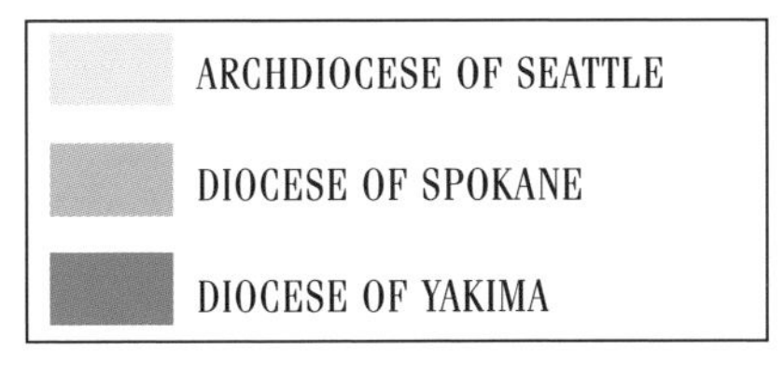

It did not matter to Blanchet that most of the people in the Oregon Country when he arrived were Native Americans. He had been a missionary among Native Americans and *Metis* in Quebec and saw no reason why Native Americans should not be part of a great Catholic culture. Blanchet approached his work with Native Americans inspired by the stories of the great missionaries in French Canada who had given their lives to spread the gospel to indigenous peoples. And he was not oblivious to the cultures of the Native Americans. In 1849, Blanchet wrote to Father Joset, the Jesuit superior in the Northwest, that he wanted to have a bishop appointed for the eastern part of the diocese because weather prevented his traveling there in winter to confirm neophytes. He went on to explain that he considered it inappropriate to expect the Native Americans to come off the hunting grounds to receive confirmation in the summer.

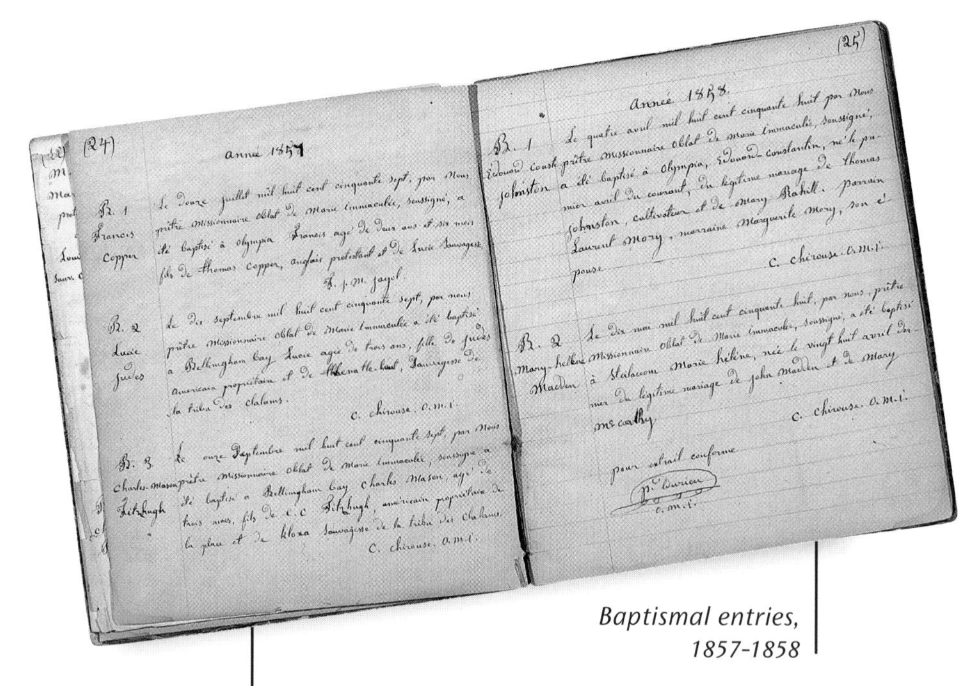

Baptismal entries, 1857-1858

If Blanchet still harbored his dream of creating an ideal French, Catholic culture when he moved to Vancouver in October of 1850, by his retirement in 1879 he knew that what he had hoped for the Native Americans had not and would not come to pass. Between 1850 and 1879, through wars, treaties, and coercion, the Native American population of Blanchet's diocese was forced onto reservations.

Blanchet and his priests, especially Brouillet, Oblates Chirouse and Pandosy, and Jesuits in the eastern part of the diocese worked tirelessly to minimize the injustices perpetrated on the Native Americans by treaty settlements and federal policy. Though bishop and priests were not immune to the ethnocentrism that characterized virtually all Europeans and Americans with regard to Native Americans, their understanding of the gospel served to mitigate some of the worst manifestations. The Church sought to provide Native Americans some protection and resources of education so that they might survive in the emerging context of the encroachment and settlement of Euro-Americans in the region.

Though Blanchet never abandoned his pastoral concern for Native Americans, and provided priests and religious for the missions and schools located among them, the growing Euro-American population increasingly absorbed his attention. Three major groups made up this population. The first was comprised of the original French-Canadian employees of the Hudson's Bay Company and their descendants. Language, culture, and extensive intermarriage among Native Americans all converged to keep these people separate from newer immigrants from the United States. Blanchet hoped to revive the piety and practice among these French-Canadians that characterized their families and friends in Quebec. In an 1863 letter to Brouillet, he instructed him to celebrate Mass alternately in the town of Walla Walla (where most of the Catholics were of Irish descent) and among the *Canadiens* and to, "Take care to teach the catechism, especially to the *Canadiens*." Blanchet saw his countrymen as a distinct group, had experienced with them prejudice at the hands of the Oregon Provisional Government, and wanted to provide pastoral care and presence to them within their own communities. The *Canadien* population of the diocese, however, did not keep pace with the growth of English-speaking Canadians, Irish, German, United States, and other mixed-European elements.

By 1850 the greatest concentration of Euro-American population centered around Fort Vancouver, Fort Nisqually, the head of Budd's Inlet where Olympia emerged, and Walla Walla. In 1850-52 new settlements were established at Port Townsend, Steilacoom, on Elliot Bay (Seattle), and on Commencement Bay (Tacoma).

Population expanded rapidly in the 1850s as people arrived attracted to the region on a quest for land, gold, and business opportunities. Continued arrivals of foreign-borns and the increase of latecomers from the mid-western and eastern United States who were being diverted from the Willamette Valley to the newly formed counties of Lewis and Clark north of the Columbia River, accounted for another increase. The Euro-American population of the Oregon Territory increased from 8,000 in 1850, the year Nesqually was established as a diocese, to 30,000 in 1855, primarily as a result of Euro-American immigration. The population boom resulted in the creation of Washington Territory in 1853.

The population figures, however, are incomplete. Native Americans, Blacks, Chinese, Filipinos, Hispanics and Pacific Islanders were

Immaculate Conception Church, Steilacoom

LaConner, 1872

CHIEF SEATTLE

Seattle was born around 1786 to a Suquamish father and a Duwamish mother at a time when the native people on the Northwest Coast were suffering the impacts of disease and culture change wrought by contact with the western world. Present as a child when George Vancouver arrived to explore Puget Sound in 1792, Seattle later gained renown for bravery and intelligence by annihilating a raiding party descending the lower White (Green) River to attack his people. He married into a noble village on Elliott Bay and had many children by several wives. Over time he became a wealthy, influential figure.

After Fort Nisqually was established in 1833, Hudson's Bay Company records described Seattle as a strikingly handsome, physically imposing leader of intimidating mien, coming often to the Fort to trade. He participated in many raids, but after a particularly violent one during which his eldest son died, he appeared to undergo a change of heart. In the late 1840's Seattle was baptized Noah Sealth (Seattle), probably by an Oblate missionary, and had his children baptized as well.

With undiminished vigor, he recruited incoming Americans to settle in his homeland and helped guide to prosperity the nascent community named after him. He was said to have assisted Bishop Demers in conducting the first Mass in Seattle on August 22, 1851.

Seattle struggled to maintain peace as settlers poured into Washington Territory, but lost the allegiance of many native people by signing the Treaty of Point Elliott. Spending the subsequent Yakima Indian War on the Fort Kitsap (Suquamish) reservation, he later reasserted his leadership, helping his people resolve disputes and mediating their relationship with American authorities. He received the sacrament of confirmation from Bishop Blanchet at St. Anne mission church at Tulalip in June 1864. On June 7, 1866, he died at Port Madison, and attended by both Catholic and native ritual, was buried near the church where he had attended Mass.

David Buerge, Seattle, WA

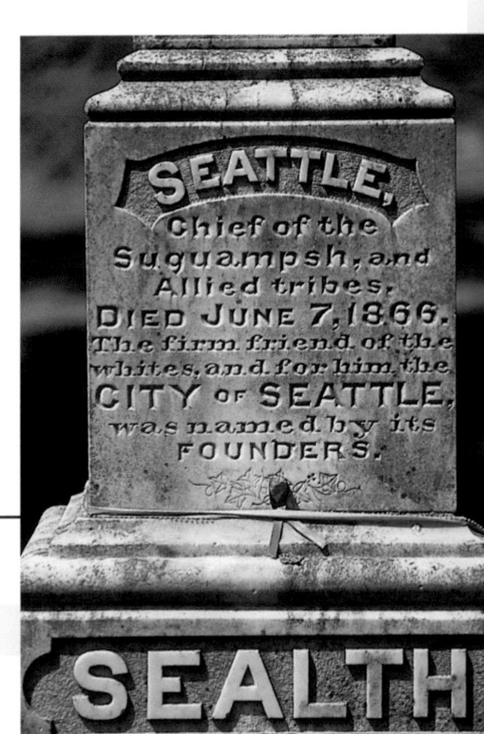

Chief Seattle's grave marker

not counted in the 1849 census. By 1880 Chinese and Japanese were counted, but the Pacific Islanders who had been a substantial presence in the Hudson's Bay Company fur trade days, were gone, having either married into Native American tribes or moved north into Canada or south into California.

The Irish entered the region during the early fur trade period, some working for the Northwest and Hudson's Bay fur companies, others arriving via the clipper trade. Irish and Irish Americans entered the Northwest in larger numbers with the Great Migration that began crossing the Oregon Trail in 1843. In 1844 a small group of immigrants settled north of the Columbia River. Among them were a Kentuckian of Irish descent, Michael T. Simmons, his wife and seven children. Simmons' family settled near present-day Tumwater along with the family of George W. Bush, a Black man barred from owning land in the Willamette Valley. The Bush and Simmons families fostered the first U.S. settlement in what is now Washington State.

The Simmons family was exceptional in that it was a family. Until the 1880s most of the Irish in Washington were single males. Irish women who were present in the region generally had non-Irish spouses, if married. The Walla Walla Valley attracted many Irish after the Civil War as did the Dublin district of Clark County. Between 1853 and 1880 the Irish in Washington clustered in Clark, King, and Walla Walla Counties, sites of military posts and mining operations. By 1880, first-generation Irish were second only to Canadians as the largest European immigrant group with 2,243 Irish listed in the 1880 census behind 2,857 Canadians. By 1890 they would be massively outnumbered by Scandinavians as well. After 1880, southern and eastern European immigrants also grew in number in Washington State.

The Quinn family, Marysville, 1883

First Communion, St. Joseph Church, Tacoma, 1916

For most European and Euro-American immigrants the mobility and opportunity of the frontier shaped profoundly the context for their lives and provided the chance for them to meet their aspirations for economic improvement. The Pacific Northwest frontier provided geographic, occupational, and social mobility for the vast majority of European immigrants until World War I. In this context these immigrants' relationship to their traditional religious institutions was weakened. To counter this danger to their faith and to provide all people in the region access to the saving grace of the Church, Blanchet strove tirelessly to set up pastoral, educational, and social service institutions that would make the church visibly present and active in his diocese. In this he was informed by a view of the Church as a supernatural institution in time that mediated God's grace to all through the sacraments.

In order to bring his vision of the Church to life, Blanchet needed resources and personnel. Financial support came primarily from Canadian and French Societies for the Propagation of the Faith, the German "Ludwig Stiftung" of Munich, and the Austrian "Leopold Stiftung" of Vienna and similar organizations. Desperately in need of funds, Blanchet departed from Vancouver on March 21, 1851 and arrived in Mexico City,

Makah salmon-fishing fleet, Neah Bay

CIRCULAR.

The Rev. Father BROUILLET, with the permission of your worthy Pastor, will have the honor to call on you and solicit your charities in behalf of the Catholic Missions of the Diocese of Nisqually, Territory of Washington Those Missions are few, struggling, and totally inadequate to the actual wants of the country Emigrants are pouring in in large numbers, generally poor; means must be provided to meet their spiritual wants. Thousands of Indians are calling earnestly for instruction and the bread of life, and hardly any one is found in the country to distribute it to them; means also must be taken to christianize and civilize those untutored and unfortunate children of nature

Arrangements have been made by the Rev. Father to take over with him a certain number of Clergymen and Sisters of Charity, with a view to provide for the more pressing necessities of those Missions; but he has not yet been able to procure the means of meeting the expenses of their journey, which must be necessarily very large, and unless he gets them somewhere, he cannot secure the above services to the Missions. n his perplexity his hope is in you, and he calls on you, confident that you will help him out of this difficulty. He solicits at your hands whatever help your generosity and your zeal for religion may prompt you to afford him, in order that he may be enabled to take with him those Clergymen and Sisters of Charity to the Missions of Washington Territory

"He that hath mercy on the poor lendeth to the Lord, and he will repay him."—Prov. xix.

Letter from A.M.A. Blanchet to Catholics in Mexico, 1851

Clockwise from center: Mother Joseph of the Sacred Heart, Sr. Praxedes of Providence, Sr. Vincent de Paul, Sr. Blandine of the Holy Angels, and Sr. Mary of the Precious Blood

May 9, 1851. He appealed to religious communities and dioceses in Mexico for support for his mission and received a generous response in the form of money as well as liturgical goods. He interrupted his trip to travel to Canada to seek sisters for the diocese and then to Baltimore to attend the First Plenary Council of Bishops in the United States. He returned to Mexico and finished his quest for financial support. On December 18, 1852, after being away almost twenty-one months, Bishop Blanchet arrived home with nearly $33,000.

Blanchet was still on his tour in Mexico when the first Sisters of Providence arrived in Oregon Country. The sisters arrived in the region at a time when the population was at its lowest ebb. Confused and discouraged, they departed for San Francisco with the Sisters of Notre Dame de Namur who had worked in the Archdiocese of Oregon City. The Providence Sisters remained in San Francisco only a short time and continued on to establish a foundation in Chile that continues today.

Blanchet requested sisters from Montreal again, in person, in 1856. Five sisters volunteered for the mission: Mother Joseph of the Sacred Heart, superior, and Sisters Praxedes of Providence, Sister Blandine of the Holy Angels and two postulants, Sisters Adelaide Theriault (Sister Vincent de Paul) and Mary Ellen Norton (Sr. Mary of the Precious Blood). The sisters, accompanied by Blanchet and Father Louis Rossi, C.P., a newly recruited priest, arrived in Vancouver on December 8, 1856.

The arrival of the sisters occasioned some conflict between Blanchet and his vicar general, J.B.A. Brouillet; conflict that reflected differing insight into the rapidly changing context of the diocese. Brouillet had been instructed to have a convent built for the sisters. He did so, but in Olympia not in Vancouver. The vicar general foresaw that growth in the western portion of the diocese would be on Puget Sound. The bishop, however, wanted the sisters in Vancouver, the oldest Euro-American population center in the diocese. On February 25, 1857, the sisters were able to move into their convent, a modest building, 16 x 24 feet. The building had four windows, a glass-paneled door, an attic that served as a dormitory, and a partitioned space that served as a chapel. Mother Joseph built the altar and tabernacle. From this space the ministry of the Sisters of Providence began and Providence Academy in Vancouver became the first parochial school in the diocese.

The sisters did not limit their work to education. Within a year they also were taking care of orphans and the infirm. Orphanages, hospitals, and homes for the elderly and disabled were established as time passed. Through the work of the sisters, the Catholic Church provided the first social welfare institutions in Washington.

For Blanchet, the wide-ranging ministry of the Providence Sisters and other religious communities was crucial to making the Church visible in the lives of people in the territory. He would repeatedly request more sisters from Montreal in order to extend Catholic presence throughout his diocese. Providing badly needed educational and social welfare services was a way of maintaining the faith of Catholics, evangelizing non-Catholics, and recruiting men and women into religious life.

By 1877, fifty-three Sisters of Providence worked in the diocese compared to seventeen priests. Numbers alone made the sisters more visible; so too did their stability compared to that of the priests who throughout Blanchet's episcopate worked primarily on the flying mission model, traveling large distances and providing pastoral care at multiple sites.

Fr. Peter J. Dubbel, Marysville

Providence multi-purpose building

Our Lady of Seven Dolors School, Tulalip

First Providence Hospital in Seattle

INTERVIEW WITH VERNON LANE

Rev. Eugene Casimir Chirouse, an Oblate priest, served the Dioceses of Walla Walla and Nesqually for 30 years. He was ordained in 1848, and in 1878 was assigned to work among the First Nations in the Fraser River valley in British Columbia until his death in 1892. Chirouse's work among the Native Americans in the Puget Sound region, particularly at the Lummi, Swinomish, Muckleshoot, Suquamish, and Tulalip reservations, left a lasting legacy with the people he served.

"In each area where there is a church, there is usually some background of Native Americans living in that area. Because when Father Chirouse came, he paddled all over and visited our communities and islands and all. There is some history about the bad things about the church not supporting the natives, but other history states that if it wasn't for the nuns and early missionaries a lot of people would have died. A lot did die, but they gave us medical help when the settlers came in with small pox. How do you put in words the hardship....

"I think the history of every reservation, every tribe, went through some struggles.... How could we stop these people from taking our land? A lot of the old warriors tried to fight, but the elders said you can't beat them, you have to learn to get along with them. That's why we are still here. We were prepared way before we even saw a white man. The old leaders said there was a new religion coming that's supposed to be better than ours – that was the Catholic missionaries.

"The biggest struggle of our people is to understand and adapt to the modern world. What we are trying to figure out is how our people are today compared to 50 years ago and how can we do it better. A lot of people are trying to understand our Catholic faith, and other faiths, but I think we are not getting to the grassroots. We need to get our kids to catechism and Church. If my entire family and my wife's family all attended church, the church as it is now, wouldn't be big enough to hold both families.

Chirouse's thurible and cross

"We aren't eating our native foods like we used to, we aren't practicing our medicine from Mother Earth, so our struggle is to be like our Lord, to give up things... We have responsibilities to ourselves, the government, to the Church... I always look at the apostles and listen to what the Lord says. He looks out for people who are lost and sick. ...it's so sad to see people fear death. Some people feel good when they have a priest anointing them or praying for them. That gives them hope. I believe in the Catholic faith—it's not a church, it's people. How do we change people to be more like Jesus and less like ourselves. The old people were a good example in a lot of ways.

"Native Americans suffered more than any minority group in America. We struggled in trying to find answers—even within the Church—to make them understand our culture and traditions, and how it was taken away, and how the Church is coming back to respecting it now, but I think you got to understand that all Indians and reservations are not the same.

"We need to study and look deeper into the history of our own people right now before it's too late, and we'll be just a thought, a memory... Where do we go from here, I don't know. We have to bring our people back together and mend all the hurts and get that forgiveness going."

The missionaries included diocesan priests, and Jesuits and Oblates who served the Native Americans in the region. The Jesuits worked in the eastern portion of the diocese, the Oblates in the middle and western portions.

The diocesan priests were charged primarily with providing pastoral services to those communities that were established or being started by Euro-American settlers. In the southeastern portion of Washington, Brouillet, at times assisted by Father Aegidius Junger, worked out of Walla Walla, serving the *Canadien* and Irish populations, the transient miners, and Native Americans, the people to whom Brouillet was most devoted.

From Vancouver, priests ministered to the surrounding areas. Father Charles Vary, assisted by Father F.X. Prefontaine in 1865, covered Cowlitz, Olympia, Seattle, Port Townsend, Whidbey Island, Port Madison, Port Gamble, and Whatcom from the town of Steilacoom. By 1867, however, Prefontaine determined that Seattle would be the population center of the Puget Sound and moved there, despite the bishop's judgment that "Seattle as a mission center was a lost cause."

Statistics provide a glimpse of the growth of the Church during Blanchet's episcopate. In 1857 there were eighteen missionaries, eight chapels and churches, and 3,918 Catholics; in 1870, thirteen missionaries, fourteen chapels and churches, and 7,000 Catholics; in 1878, fifteen missionaries, twenty-two churches and chapels, and 12,000 Catholics. Eleven Providence Sisters served in the diocese in 1861, Fifty-three were serving by 1877.

Tulalip

Blanchet retired in 1879 and spent his remaining years in Vancouver, where he died in February, 1887. He retired praying that those in the region who followed him would, "...have the pleasure of seeing mature the good seed, which has been scattered in this garden of God during the past forty years."

Blanchet's successor was Aegidius Junger, born and raised in Germany, who had come from the American College at Louvain, Belgium, as a young priest to work as a missionary in the Diocese of Nesqually in the early 1860s. Bishop Junger served from 1879 to 1895, a period of rapid population increase occasioned by the completion of the railroad link between the east and Puget Sound. By the time of Junger's death, the Euro-American population of the diocese would increase from 75,000 to nearly 400,000 people, distributed over a territory of almost 70,000 square miles. The Catholic population

Aegidius Junger

Confirmation picnic, Port Angeles, Bishop Junger at left, 1895

St. Mary Church, McGowan

during this same period increased from 12,000 to 42,000. The number of churches and public chapels increased from twenty-three to eighty-two. Diocesan clergy increased from ten to thirty-eight, not including the twenty-four priests of religious orders engaged in pastoral work in the diocese.

The number of women religious in the diocese increased from approximately sixty to 286. This number included 148 Sisters of Providence as well as twenty-seven Sisters of the Holy Names of Jesus and Mary, who had begun working in the diocese in 1880; thirty-five Benedictine women located in Tacoma and Uniontown, the second group having arrived in 1887; thirty-three Sisters of St. Francis of Philadelphia; at least two Sisters of St. Dominic; eight Sisters of St. Joseph of Peace (Newark); seven Sisters of the Good Shepherd; and twenty-three Sisters of the Visitation. In addition, Dominican Sisters staffed a hospital in Aberdeen beginning in 1890 and Sisters of St. Francis of Glen Riddle an orphanage in Spokane beginning in 1890.

Sacred Heart School, Seattle, with Sr. Dominica Ryan, O.P.

Pioneer priests with Bp. Junger (last row, center), Vancouver

The only male religious community active in the diocese when Junger began his episcopate was the Jesuits whose work in Spokane, Colville, and points east, nurtured the faith among Native Americans and Euro-Americans alike. During Junger's tenure, new religious communities entered the diocese. The Redemptorists came to Seattle in 1891. The Benedictines arrived in 1891 to serve German-speaking Catholics in the Tacoma area. Shortly thereafter they began to build St. Martin's Abbey and College in Lacey.

Junger inherited the shortage of resources and personnel and the challenges to be met by a shifting and mobile population. He lacked sufficient numbers of priests to minister to all the Catholics coming into the region. The immigrants, for their part, were preoccupied with making a better life. While they wanted the Church for the major life-cycle sacraments, supporting clergy and a parish community was not at the top of

St. Anne Church, Tulalip

their agendas as they moved around looking for better land, better work, better mines.

Junger also built a new St. James Cathedral. Construction began on July 27, 1884, and was completed in 1885. The brick and stone building was 60 x 140 feet and cost $50,000.00. These costs put the diocese into a debt which haunted the bishop.

First marriage at SS. Peter & Paul Church, Tacoma, 1894

St. James Cathedral, Vancouver, dedicated 1885

First holy Communion at Our Lady of Lourdes Church, Wilkeson

Using the limited resources at his disposal, Junger worked steadily to provide pastoral presence and Catholic educational and social welfare institutions in stable population centers where a sufficient number of settled Catholics would be able to support them. Most of the churches built were simple wooden structures because of scarce resources, yet they were sacred spaces where Catholics could celebrate Mass and receive the sacraments. Junger was kindly and loved by his priests and people. Sometimes he would take up his violin during Mass and provide music for the service. The bishop carried a heavy burden, trying to provide pastoral presence and care with perpetually insufficient financial and personnel resources. Worn down by these cares, Junger died at Vancouver on December 26, 1895. The second bishop of the Diocese of Nesqually, Aegidius Junger was the only one born and raised in Europe.

St. John Vianney Church, Darrington

Bishops Blanchet and Junger stand as two of the great missionaries of the diocese. A French-Canadian and a German, the first leaders of the Church in Washington State - between them they led the Church during a period of rapid, convulsive change. Junger died as the economic depression following the Great Panic of 1893 deepened, signaling more difficulties and change for the diocese under its new leader, the U.S.-born and Pacific Northwest-raised Edward O'Dea.

St. Francis Xavier Cemetery, Toledo

Sacred Heart Church, Winlock

St. Joseph Church and School, Chehalis

Chapter 2

AMERICANIZING AN IMMIGRANT CHURCH ON A WANING FRONTIER

1896-1918

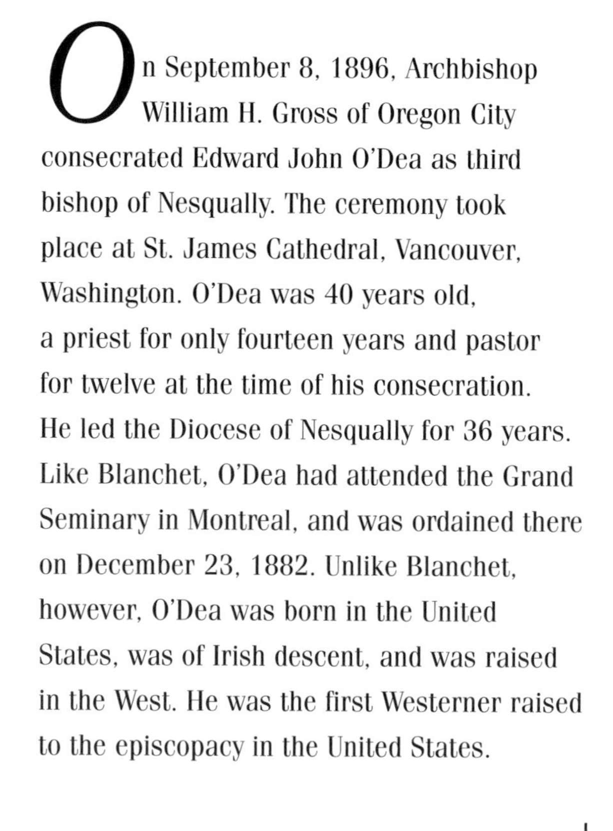

On September 8, 1896, Archbishop William H. Gross of Oregon City consecrated Edward John O'Dea as third bishop of Nesqually. The ceremony took place at St. James Cathedral, Vancouver, Washington. O'Dea was 40 years old, a priest for only fourteen years and pastor for twelve at the time of his consecration. He led the Diocese of Nesqually for 36 years. Like Blanchet, O'Dea had attended the Grand Seminary in Montreal, and was ordained there on December 23, 1882. Unlike Blanchet, however, O'Dea was born in the United States, was of Irish descent, and was raised in the West. He was the first Westerner raised to the episcopacy in the United States.

Edward John O'Dea

Clergy gathered for O'Dea's installation, Vancouver, 1896

O'Dea's episcopate spanned the end of the frontier period for Puget Sound. He led the diocese through economic turmoil, massive population increases, anti-Catholic social movements, World War I, and into the Great Depression. When he died on Christmas Day, 1932, on the 50th anniversary of his ordination to the priesthood, O'Dea had succeeded in transforming the Diocese of Nesqually from a European immigrant, frontier diocese into a diocese of the U.S. Catholic Church, the Diocese of Seattle.

O'Dea inherited from Junger a missionary diocese with about 42,000 Catholics, forty-two churches with resident priests, sixty-nine priests (diocesan and religious), and 263 women religious scattered through an area of 70,000 square miles, what is today the entire state of Washington. When O'Dea died in 1932, the Diocese of Seattle, now less than half the state geographically, had approximately 100,000 Catholics, 113 diocesan and 119 religious order priests, 1031 women religious, and eighty-nine churches with resident pastors.

At the beginning of his episcopate, O'Dea traveled by stage and horseback throughout his diocese to administer the sacrament of confirmation, encourage and counsel his priests, and visit the women engaged in a range of educational, health-care and charitable work.

D.H. Hanley, Columbia Valley

Confirmation at St. Peter Mission, Suquamish, 1916

St. Mary Church, Pioneer

On one visit to missions in the Big Bend area, O'Dea decided to take with him the choir from the parish in Cheney, one of the few choirs in eastern Washington. Believing that their singing would enliven services at the missions, he loaded the choir and its ancient portable organ in a light spring wagon for the trip. Thirty years later, Bishop O'Dea traveled by train and automobile to visit the same parishes and missions.

Peter Hylebos

O'Dea became bishop of Nesqually in the midst of an economic depression in the United States. In June, a financial panic that had begun on the East Coast shook the Northwest. Financial institutions collapsed, including five banks in Spokane and fourteen in Tacoma. Both the Union Pacific and the Northern Pacific railroads, serving the Northwest, went bankrupt. Unemployment levels were high; the homeless on Puget Sound huddled in makeshift shacks and lived on wild berries and clams. Even those workers who did not lose their jobs had wages cut by as much as 20%. In an annual report for the year 1898, Peter Hylebos, pastor of St. Leo Parish, Tacoma, noted that the poor boxes had been "robbed about ten times" and that he had given "more than one hundred dollars of my own money" to the poor.

The situation of the 1890s, aggravated by downturns in 1896 and 1897, lent a certain irony to the words of a song popular among settlers in Western Washington at that time:

And now that I'm used to the climate,
I think that if man ever found
A spot to live easy and happy,
That Eden is on Puget Sound.
No longer the slave of ambition
I laugh at the world and its shams,
As I think of my pleasant condition,
Surrounded by acres of clams.

Given the situation, it is no wonder that the Klondike gold strike of 1897-98 attracted many from Washington State. Hylebos expressed the consequence of such a fluid economic life for his parish by describing the number of parishioners

Duwamish River tideflats

in his parish as, "They come and go—impossible to keep track," and the number of parish societies as being, ...only in quasi existence, too many members left for the mine, and other diggings."

O'Dea was faced with the task of stabilizing the finances of his diocese. Money he needed to build churches for the ever increasing number of Catholic immigrants in the area was scanty. Further, a $25,000 mortgage foreclosure threatened the Cathedral in Vancouver. O'Dea appealed to his priests for help with the mortgage at the first diocesan synod. The priests and their people responded and immediately pledged enough money to wipe out the debt.

Pressed by financial problems throughout his entire episcopate, O'Dea boldly went forward planning for the organization of new parishes, encouraging and overseeing the building of churches, hospitals, and schools, and stimulating the development of spiritual life through parish missions, retreats for laymen, and a wide range of

Construction, Mt. St. Vincent, Seattle, 1923

Priests' retreat, St. Martin's Abbey, Lacey, 1914

devotional practices. He was confident in his understanding of buildings and a skilled reader of blueprint designs, something he had learned from Mother Joseph.

Our Lady of Good Help Church and F. X. Prefontaine, Seattle

O'Dea saw, as Brouillet, A.M.A. Blanchet's vicar general had predicted earlier, that the population and economic center of the diocese was Puget Sound. The demographic and economic realities of the Hudson's Bay Company period that had made Vancouver the premier city had changed radically. Now Seattle was the center. The city's population had increased from 3,553 in 1880 to 42,837 in 1890. By 1900 it had nearly doubled to 80,871. By 1920 Seattle's population would reach 315,312. O'Dea moved to Seattle in 1903, announcing the move from the pulpit of Our Lady of Good Help Church, the first Catholic Church in the city.

In November, 1905, the cornerstone was laid for the new St. James Cathedral and on December 22, 1907, it was dedicated. During the Mass, the change of the name of the diocese, from Nesqually to Seattle, was announced. Seattle had four Catholic parishes when O'Dea moved to the

St. James Cathedral, Seattle, pre-1916

city in 1903. By the time of his death in 1932, the city had twenty-six. O'Dea's goal from the beginning of his episcopate was to "have churches within reach of all his people." In addition to churches, construction of schools, hospitals, and orphanages continued apace.

In 1913 O'Dea recommended to Rome that a second diocese be created in Washington State, an action he considered necessary because of population growth. His recommendation was accepted and on December 17, 1913, the Diocese of Spokane was created with the line of division running north and south, nearly coincident with the 120th meridian, and the north to south course of the Columbia River. The Vatican's decision was announced in April, 1914.

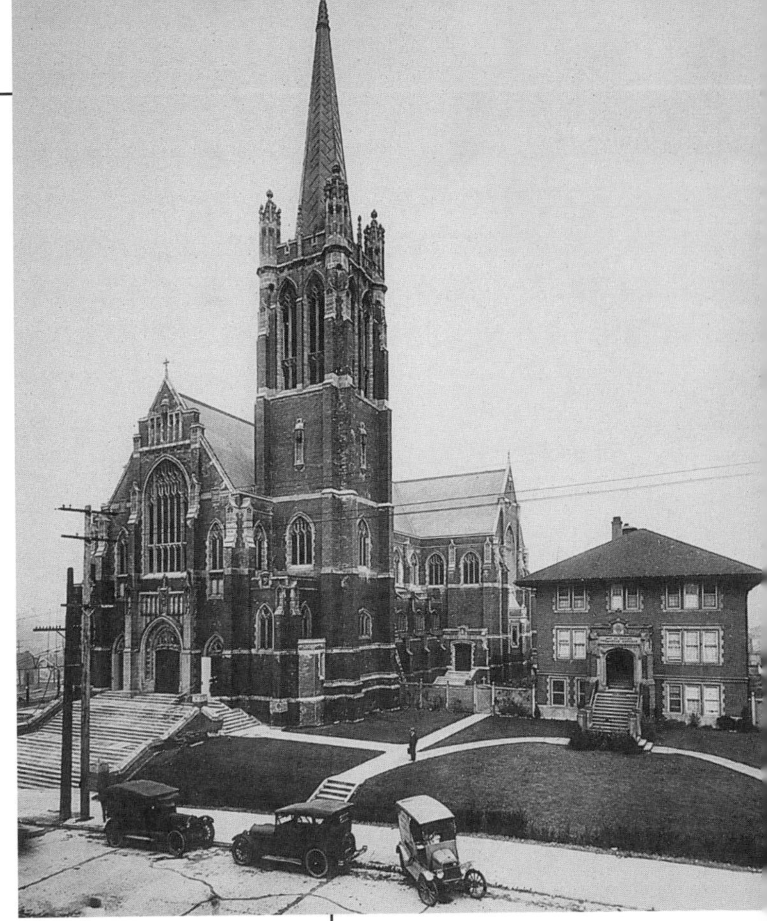

Blessed Sacrament Church, Seattle, 1925

St. Helen's Hospital, Chehalis

St. Helens Hospital, Chehalis, Wash.

CHEHALIS

Washington's population increased four-fold from the time of O'Dea's consecration in 1896 until his death in 1932, from nearly 400,000 to nearly 1,600,000. Much of this new population came to Washington via the trans-continental railroad. These new immigrants left a distinctive mark on Washington State. They outnumbered the pioneer generation so significantly that they eventually took power and influence.

In 1900 Washington had a higher percentage of foreign-born residents than the U.S. as a whole. The majority of immigrants came from Scandinavia (Norway, Sweden, Iceland, and Denmark), Great Britain, Canada, and Germany and were referred to as the "old immigrants." In the opening decades of the 20th century the "new immigrants" arrived—peoples from southern and eastern Europe. As well, the character of Asian immigration changed. The Japanese population grew at a much greater rate than the Chinese. Some immigrant groups arrived as families but, as had historically been the case, more groups were comprised largely of single men looking for work. Mexican immigrants also increased in number, adding to a Mexican population that had been present and growing since

St. Teresa Residence lobby, staffed by the Sisters of St. Joseph of Peace

Briscoe Memorial School for Boys, Kent

the Hudson's Bay Company days. Miners from Sonora, Mexico as well as Chileans and Peruvians took part in the gold rush in the inland Northwest during the 1860s and continued to take part in the strikes throughout the Pacific Northwest, including British Columbia and Alaska. In the early 20th century Mexicans and Mexican-American migrants began to supply field labor for the expanding agricultural industry in Washington State.

Church of the Assumption, Bellingham

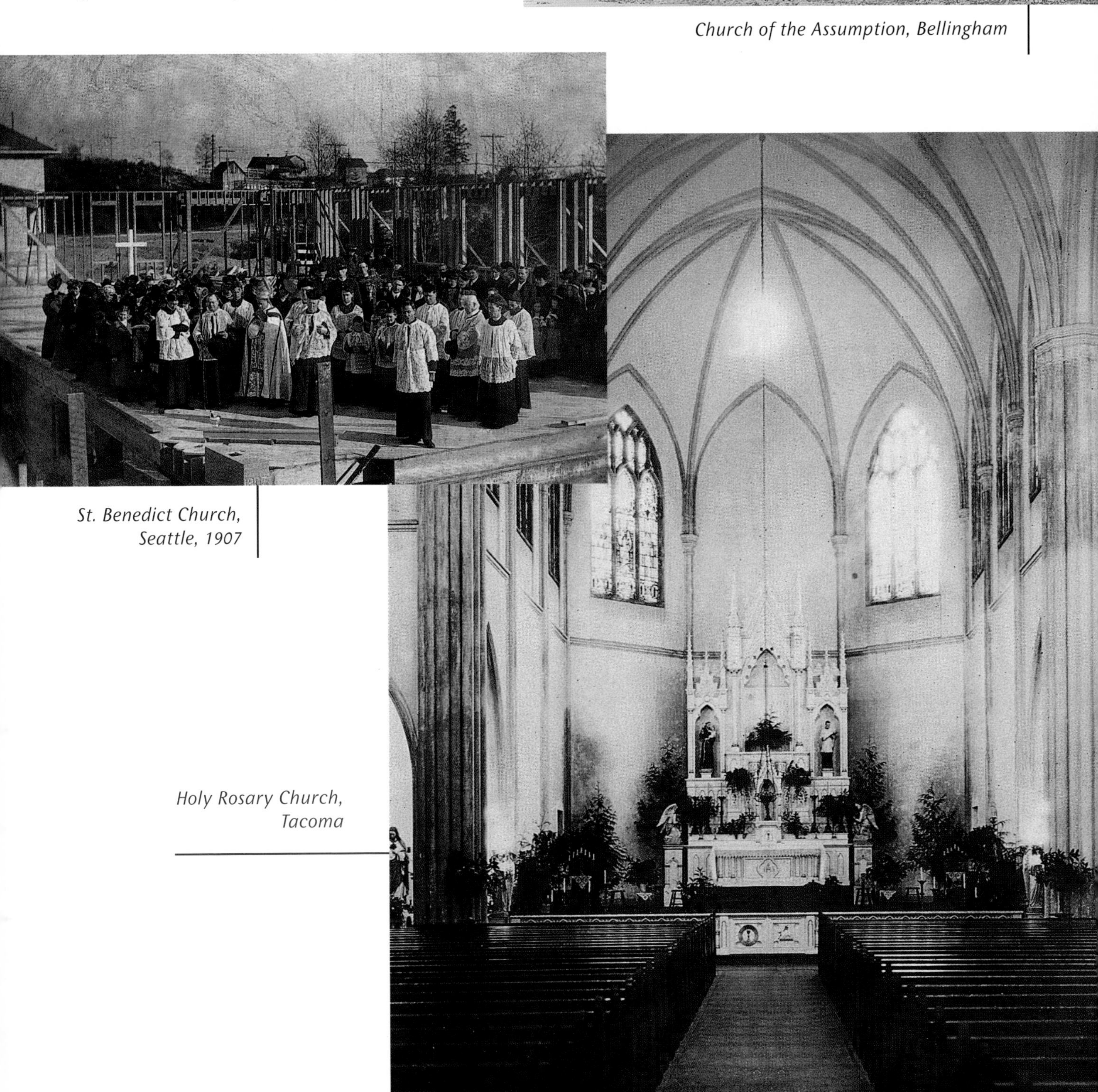

St. Benedict Church, Seattle, 1907

Holy Rosary Church, Tacoma

Sacred Heart Parish, LaConner, 1899. l-r: W.J. Metz, Bishop O'Dea, F.X. Prefontaine

Francis Moens (l), St. Mary Church, Pioneer

Washington became a destination for new immigrants, often because its topographics and economies were recognizable in relation to those of their home cultures. Hence Scandinavians clustered in Puget Sound: Swedes lumbered and logged; Norwegians and Finns fished; Danes engaged in dairy farming. The Irish worked in construction, mining, and agriculture. The Italians farmed, the Greeks entered the region as railroad laborers. Seattle had a thriving foreign-language press in the early 20th century.

Newspapers were published in Swedish, Norwegian, Italian, Japanese, and German. Chinese- and Japanese-language papers were published as well beginning in the 1890s. Basques settled in the Yakima Valley. In eastern Washington ethnic communities gravitated to agriculture. The Italians prospered as farmers in the Walla Walla Valley, and became famous for sweet onions. Germans established farming settlements in eastern Washington, as did some Irish.

St. Rita Church, Tacoma

The Italian immigration to Washington was the impetus for Missionary Sisters of the Sacred Heart to begin work in Seattle in 1903. St. Frances Xavier Cabrini arrived in Seattle in the fall of that year. From their Mt. Carmel Mission on Beacon Hill, the sisters visited the poor, the sick, the imprisoned, and those who had drifted away from the faith. In March they opened a school from which grew Our Lady of Mt. Virgin School and Church. In 1918 the sisters moved to a site on Lake Washington. In 1915, Cabrini purchased the Perry Hotel which became Columbus Hospital and received its first patients in 1916. Sacred Heart Orphanage was erected in 1924 and St. Paul's Infant Home in 1929. These institutions provided care to orphaned and abandoned children, the casualties of the physical and economic misfortunes that beset many immigrants to the region.

St. Frances Xavier Cabrini

St. Paul's Infant Home/Sacred Heart Orphanage, Seattle

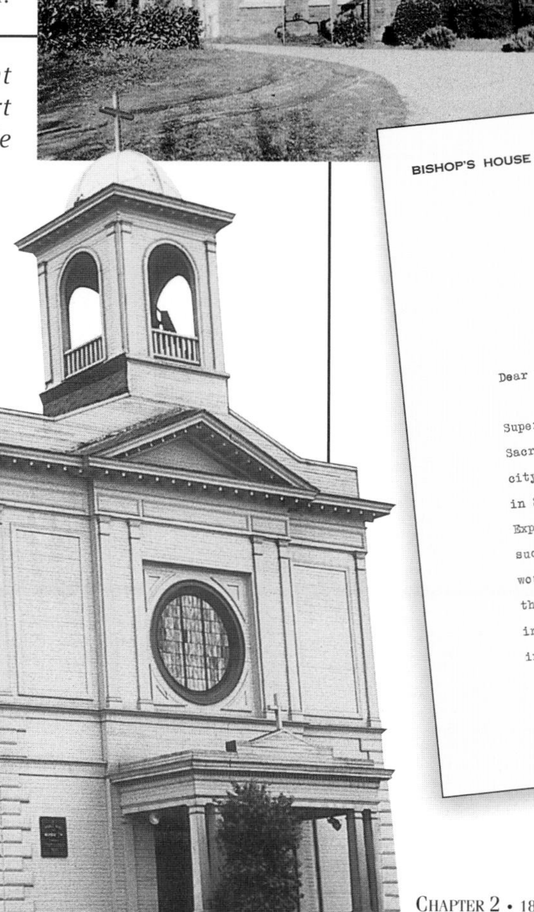

Our Lady of Mount Virgin Church, Seattle

BISHOP'S HOUSE

804 NINTH AVENUE
SEATTLE
Sept. 7, 1915.

Dear Rev. Father:

Very Rev. Mother F. X. Cabrini, Foundress and Superior General of the Missionary Sisters of the Sacred Heart of Jesus, has recently arrived in this city from New York for the purpose of establishing in Seattle a foundling institution or "Babies Home". Experience, no doubt, has taught you how greatly such an institution is needed in this diocese and I would therefore feel obliged to you for announcing this undertaking to your parishioners and for encouraging them to aid the Very Rev. Mother or her Sisters in this very necessary and urgent charity.

Yours faithfully in Christ,

Bishop of Seattle.

Letter from O'Dea regarding Mother Cabrini

Other women religious communities that entered the Diocese of Seattle while O'Dea was bishop included: the Carmelite Nuns (1908), Sisters of Charity of St. Vincent de Paul (1927), Sisters of the Society of the Divine Savior (1899), Religious of the Sacred Heart (1908), the Sisters of Charity of the Blessed Virgin Mary (1921), the Ursulines (1911), the Lady Catechists (1913), the Sisters of St. Ann (1928), the Little Daughters of St. Joseph (1932), the Maryknoll Sisters (1920), the Sisters of the Immaculate Heart of Mary (1907), and the Sisters of St. Francis of Penance (1911). These sisters joined the already significant number of women religious who had been coming to the diocese since 1856.

The history of the Sisters of Providence illustrates how women religious constructed and expanded health care, social service, and educational institutions in the state and for Catholics. In Vancouver they operated a boarding and day school beginning in 1857; a home for the mentally disturbed from 1857 to 1868; St. Joseph's Hospital from 1858; and St. Vincent's Orphanage for Boys and St. Genevieve's Orphanage for girls from 1861 to 1923.

Beginning in 1875, the sisters expanded their work beyond Vancouver and the Tulalip Indian missions and rapidly erected more hospitals, including: Providence, Seattle (1877); St. Mary's, Walla Walla (1880); Sacred Heart, Spokane (1886); St. Peter's Olympia (1887); St. John's, Port Townsend (1890); and St. Elizabeth's, Yakima (1891). In Seattle, between 1888 and 1895, Sisters Blandine, Peter Claver, and Aegidius headed a program of social service that served over 60,000 meals to the poor and made more than 5,000 visits to the poor and sick not in the hospital.

In addition to their health care ministry the Providence sisters engaged extensively in educational ministry in the diocese. Until the arrival of the Sisters of the Holy Names of Jesus and Mary they were the only sisters teaching in the diocese. Providence Academy, Vancouver

Providence Academy, Vancouver

Female students of Our Lady of Seven Dolors School, Tulalip

(1856); St. Vincent Academy, Walla Walla (1864); St. Amable (now St. Michael), Olympia (1881); and St. Joseph Academy, Yakima (1875) were some of the first institutions to be established. From 1863 to 1875 the sisters were at St. Joseph Academy, Steilacoom; Our Lady of Lourdes Academy, Cowlitz (1876-1898) and Our Lady of Seven Dolors School for Indians, Tulalip (1868-1901). The last was the first contract Indian school in the United States.

The Sisters of Providence were the only women religious in the diocese providing health care until 1888 when the Sisters of St. Francis came to work at St. George Indian School. In 1891 the Order established St. Joseph Hospital, Tacoma. In 1921 the Franciscans took over the Catholic Federation of Tacoma's St. Ann Day Home and it became St. Ann Receiving Home which cared for infants, unwed mothers, and orphaned and abandoned girls.

St. George Indian School, Tacoma, with the Sisters of St. Francis of Philadelphia

In 1890 the Sisters of St. Joseph arrived in Bellingham and established St. Joseph Hospital which opened its doors in 1891. The Sisters of the Holy Names of Jesus and Mary arrived in Seattle at the request of Father Prefontaine in 1880. They opened Holy Names Academy, the first Catholic school for girls in Seattle.

St. Joseph Hospital, Bellingham

In 1894 they took on teaching responsibilities at Sacred Heart Parish School, in 1906 at the School of the Immaculate, and in 1907, St. Joseph School for boys only. In 1923 they took on teaching at three new parochial schools in Seattle: St. Anne, St. Mary, and St. Patrick.

The stories of all the communities of women religious are important to understanding the history of the Archdiocese of Seattle, though there is not sufficient space to include each individually. Women religious outnumbered priests nearly five to one for over seventy-five years in the diocese. Besides providing essential services, these women were living symbols of Catholic belief, practice, and community. For immigrants in a new land and for people distracted from the faith by the promise of wealth and the opportunities and challenges of constant mobility,

Holy Names Academy, Seattle

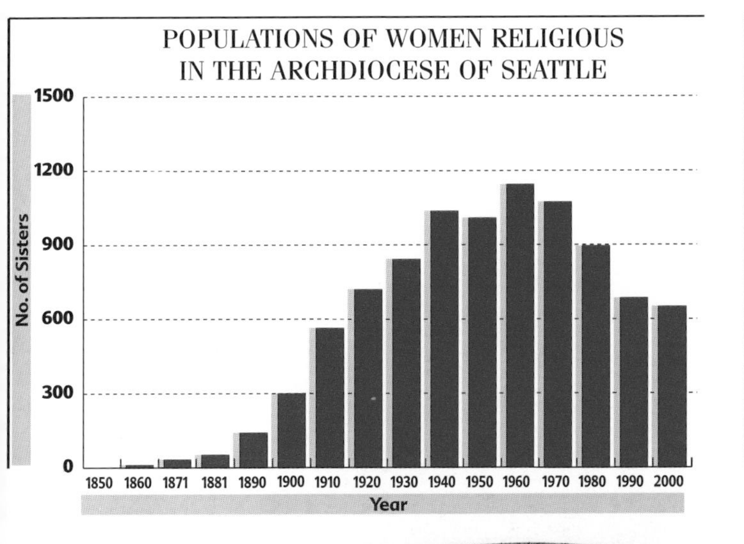

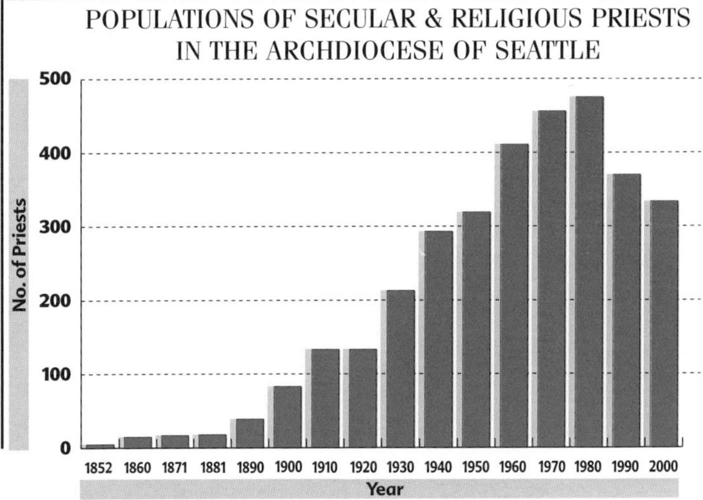

St. Joseph School, Seattle

women religious stood as a significant connection, for some a lifeline to the Catholic faith of their families and cultures in Europe, Canada, or the eastern United States. The sisters made real a Catholic heritage that easily could be lost in the disorienting experiences that were part and parcel of migration.

The growth of Catholic institutions and personnel and the growing numbers of Catholics who were putting down roots in cities, towns, or farming communities, led to the growth of organizations among laity. Two organizations found in virtually every parish were the Altar Society for women and the Holy Name Society for men.

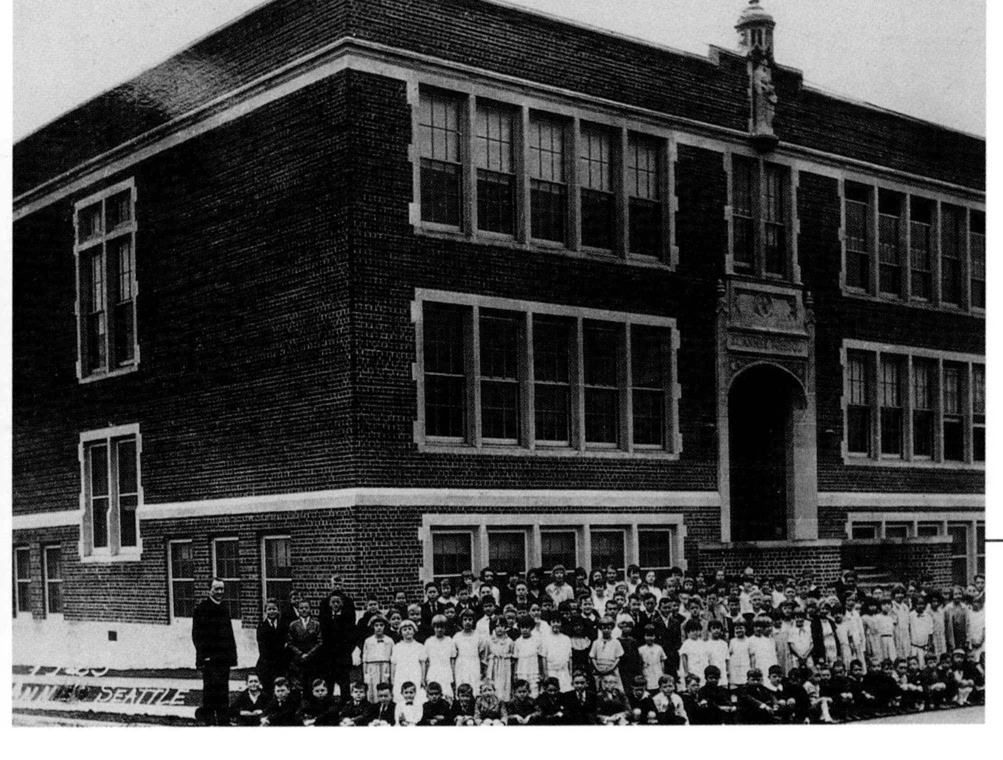

St. Ann School, Seattle

Holy Name Society picnic

Gentlemen's Sodality of the B.V.M. badge

Ladies' Altar Society of the B.V.M. badge

The Altar Society cared for the altar cloths and vestments of the parish and the upkeep of the altar and sacristy area. The members also met monthly for Mass and Communion. They provided socials to encourage community among women in the parish, usually combining conviviality with fundraising in these events.

The Holy Name Society, first established in the diocese at Our Lady of Good Help Church in Seattle in 1909, provided socializing and monthly Mass and communion for men. The society's purpose was to counter cursing, swearing, and blasphemy with prayer, especially recitation of the Divine Praises in honor of God's Holy Name.

Holy Family Church, Auburn

Knights of Columbus, St. James Church, Vancouver

By 1917 the Holy Name Society in Seattle had extended itself into anti-pornography campaigns, especially improving moving pictures shown in the city, and programs for distribution of Catholic literature in Catholic homes and schools. The Society was responsible for getting *The Catholic Encyclopedia* placed on the shelves of the Seattle Public Library along with other Catholic books. This society also sponsored the Catholic Boy Scouts and the original sports programs out of which grew the CYO or Catholic Youth Organization. O'Dea saw the Holy Name Society as an organization of men who were to "go forth before the world and win it for Christ and his holy religion by example of good and consistent Catholic living." Members were to "show what Catholic men are."

The Catholic Society, St. Barbara Church, Black Diamond

Between 1875 and 1910 most of the lay organizations found in any parish tended to be fraternal insurance societies. These were the origins of the Young Men's Institute, which entered the diocese in the 1890s; the Young Ladies' Institute, which entered the diocese in 1905; the Knights of Columbus, which came into the diocese in 1902; the Catholic Daughters of America, which came into the diocese in 1910; and the Catholic Order of Foresters and its Ladies' Auxiliary, which entered the diocese in the second decade of the 20th century. The primary function of these societies was the provision of sickness and death benefits to members. These organizations reflected the tenuous quality of life in the 19th century. These organizations were an "Americanization" of the fraternal societies organized by ethnic group, for example the Central Verein for the Germans, the Ancient Order of Hibernians for the Irish, and similar organizations for the Italians, Portuguese, and other ethnic groups. The new organizations appealed to all Catholic ethnic groups for membership, promoted Catholic over ethnic identity, and urged Catholics to be good citizens and good parishioners. This Americanizing was conveyed in the motto of the Young Men's Institute, *"Pro Deo, Pro Patria"* (For God, For Country). These groups wanted to reduce the gap between Catholics and the United States and to protect Catholic interests in the nation. O'Dea encouraged all these organizations as venues for strengthening the faith of the laity, and for making them loyal to the church and their country over their ethnic identities.

Mother's Day procession, 1926

William J. Noonan (left of O'Dea) with St. James Cathedral Usher Society

As Catholics became more settled and more economically affluent, the older societies began to function primarily as social and charitable organizations. New organizations were formed for the same purpose. The Diocesan Council of Catholic Women (DCCW) was organized in the diocese in 1921. The purpose of the council was to unite the many women's groups in Catholic parishes into a federation for more effective action. The goal was to harness the coordinated energy of these groups to undertake projects of diocesan or general interest. The first activities the bishop wanted the DCCW to undertake were support of the Newman Clubs at the University of Washington, the normal schools at Ellensburg and Bellingham, study clubs, Catholic Parent Teacher Associations, rural religious aid, and immigrant aid and Americanization. The DCCW harnessed the economic affluence and social status of middle-class and wealthy Catholic women as a lever to bring immigrants to a higher level.

A major venue for lay involvement in charitable work was The Society of St. Vincent de Paul. Officially organized in the diocese on January 26, 1920, charitable work had been going on at least at the Church of the Immaculate since 1893 under the name of the Immaculate Conception Association of Charity. The first official conference of the Society was organized in St. Benedict Parish. In a year the organization had grown enough that the Seattle Council had to be organized. In 1924 a separate council was organized in Tacoma. The Salvage Bureau was the Society's best known activity.

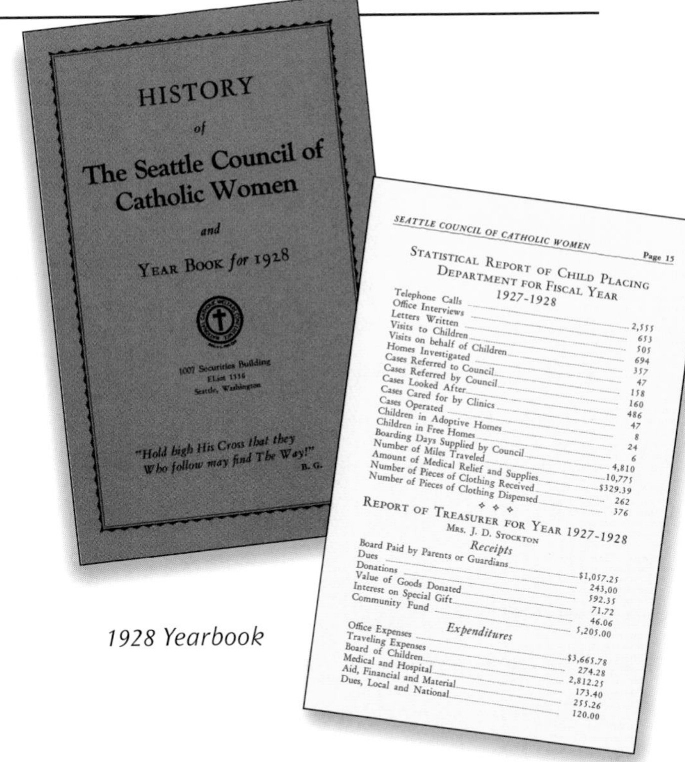
HISTORY

of

The Seattle Council of Catholic Women

and

Year Book for 1928

1007 Securities Building
Eliot 1316
Seattle, Washington

"Hold high His Cross that they
Who follow may find The Way!"
B. G.

SEATTLE COUNCIL OF CATHOLIC WOMEN — Page 15

Statistical Report of Child Placing Department for Fiscal Year 1927-1928

Telephone Calls	2,555
Office Interviews	653
Letters Written	505
Visits to Children	694
Visits on behalf of Children	357
Homes Investigated	47
Cases Referred to Council	158
Cases Referred by Council	160
Cases Looked After	486
Cases Cared for by Clinics	47
Cases Operated	8
Children in Adoptive Homes	24
Children in Free Homes	6
Boarding Days Supplied by Council	4,810
Number of Miles Traveled	10,775
Amount of Medical Relief and Supplies	$329.39
Number of Pieces of Clothing Received	262
Number of Pieces of Clothing Dispensed	376

Report of Treasurer for Year 1927-1928
Mrs. J. D. Stockton

Receipts

Board Paid by Parents or Guardians	$1,057.25
Dues	243,00
Donations	592.35
Value of Goods Donated	71.72
Interest on Special Gift	46.06
Community Fund	5,205.00

Expenditures

Office Expenses	$3,665.78
Traveling Expenses	274.28
Board of Children	2,812.25
Medical and Hospital	173.40
Aid, Financial and Material	255.26
Dues, Local and National	120.00

1928 Yearbook

Other organizations for laity had spiritual growth as their primary purpose. A group of Catholic students at the University of Washington banded together on the anniversary of the conversion of John Henry Cardinal Newman,

Catholic Federation of Western Washington, an association of benevolent and charitable societies, 1923

Monstrance

October 9, 1908, to found the Seattle Chapter of the Newman Club. The Newman Club's purpose was to educate students in the spiritual life and to bring Christ to the campus. Under the tutelage of priest theologians and the mentorship of active Catholic faculty on the campus, the Newman Club sought to join university students' faith with their academic pursuits.

In 1918, O'Dea blessed the initiation of the Laymen's retreat movement in the diocese. Ninety men gathered at St. Martin's College, Lacey, for a few days of prayer and meditation in a directed personal spiritual inventory. The retreat was sponsored by the Knights of Columbus and approved by O'Dea. The retreats continued annually thereafter. While no comparable retreat movement for women was instituted, by the 1920s there were retreat opportunities for women in houses of women religious in the diocese.

A range of parish-based confraternities and sodalities grew as well, including: the Holy Angels Society, Boys Sanctuary, Children of Mary, St. John Berchman's Sodality, Sodality of Mary, and the League of the Sacred Heart, which was promoted especially in Jesuit parishes. These organizations encouraged private and communal prayer and living a pious life. Most parishes provided groups for married men, married women, young women, young men, boys, girls, single men, and single

Immaculate Conception Church, Seattle

women. Each was geared to a specific age, sex, and marital status. Each group, usually meeting monthly, provided an occasion for instruction in Catholic belief and practice.

Annual parish missions also continued to be part of Catholic life in the diocese as they had from its earliest days. A mission now lasted for a week with sermons each night for a different age group and gender of the parish population. The week of preaching, prayer, and sacraments, particularly confession and the urging to frequent communion, especially by 1920, reinforced Catholic identity and inspired Catholic devotion and regular practice. Missions were well attended because they also were social events. A major focus of missions was Benediction of the Blessed Sacrament. This rite, with silence, song, candles, darkness, and the opportunity for people to gaze on the Body of Christ created an aura of awe. Benediction, for many faithful, was an experience of intense intimacy with Christ as the priest blessed the people with the Real Presence visible to them in the monstrance.

Another milestone in the cementing of Catholic institutions in the diocese came in 1911 when O'Dea took over the *Catholic Northwest Progress* as the official diocesan newspaper. The roots of this paper went back into the 1890s when Martina Johnston began a periodical called the *Catholic Northwest.* In March, 1899 the Seattle Council of the Young Men's Institute established a monthly called the *Progress.* O'Dea endorsed the publication in 1901. In 1908 the two periodicals merged and Johnston became the editor. The goals of the combined publication were the education of Catholics, defense of the faith, and the social uplifting of Catholics, especially newer immigrants. In May of 1911 the paper was reorganized as the *Northwest Progress Company* and became the official organ for the diocese.

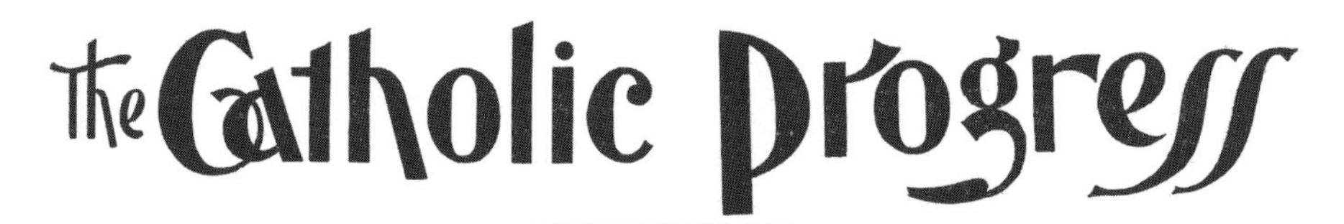

1900

1910

DO THIS TODAY
The Advertisers in This Paper Are Your Friends—You Can Be Sure of That—Then Patronize Them

VOL. XXVI—NO. 44. SEATTLE, WASHINGTON, NOVEMBER 7, 1924. $2.00 PER YEAR

1924

Martina Johnston continued as editor with a salary of $75 per month. She was given "...full control and supervision in the writing and arrangement of the First and Editorial Page of the *Catholic North West Progress*, and that the management and control of the remaining part of the said paper above mentioned be vested absolutely in the management of the corporation." Johnston remained editor of the *Progress* until April 17, 1914, when Edward J. Coen took over.

Johnston was the first of four women whose leadership and editorial skill would shape the paper in significant ways. Ethel Egan worked for eleven years at the paper, beginning in 1915, substituting frequently for managing editor, William O'Connell. O'Connell, who had joined the paper as an assistant in 1914, took over as editor in 1918, a position he would hold until his death in 1959. Mary Bresnahan joined the paper in 1925 working as a reporter, later managing editor, and retiring as associate editor in 1972. Kay Lagreid joined the paper in 1970. In 1978 she was appointed managing editor of the *Progress*, One of only eight women editing diocesan newspapers in the U.S. Lagreid continues to work at the paper in editorial and reporting capacities.

Bishop O'Dea's paper struggled and many questioned its official status. In November 1911, he issued an official letter to be read at all masses announcing that the *Catholic Northwest Progress* was the only official Catholic paper authorized and approved. O'Dea urged people to support the paper as the official diocesan organ which served as "an authoritative medium of communication in official announcement."

O'Dea had been in office nearly twenty-one years when the U.S. entered World War I in 1917. The United States' entry into the war constituted

Holy Cross Church, Taylor

Knights of Columbus, Fort Lewis

yet another phase in the Americanization of an immigrant Catholic Church. An entire page of the *Progress* was given over to government bulletins and the size of the paper was limited to help the war effort. Catholic soldiers and chaplains from the region were covered with patriotism and encouragement. The wounding and deaths of young men were noted, often as part of articles underscoring the efforts of popes to obtain peace. Young Catholic men were encouraged to volunteer and later to cooperate with the draft. Serving their country in war was presented in churches as a religious responsibility.

Sermons, *Progress* articles, and parish activities during the war were designed to show to themselves and to the world around them that Catholics were good Americans. For their Protestant neighbors the question was a very real one, given the large number of immigrants and children of immigrants in the Catholic churches of Seattle.

At the end of World War I, O'Dea led a diocese much larger, more urban, and more industrial than the one he had taken over from Junger. He had expanded Catholic institutions and personnel, encouraged lay organizations and piety, and managed to keep the diocese running despite almost constant fiscal difficulties. His dream, the mark that in O'Dea's mind would demonstrate the maturity of his diocese, was to establish a seminary. He clung to that dream during the challenges of the 1920s.

Seattle waterfront

Chapter 3

NEW CHALLENGES FOR AN EXPANDING CHURCH, 1918-1929

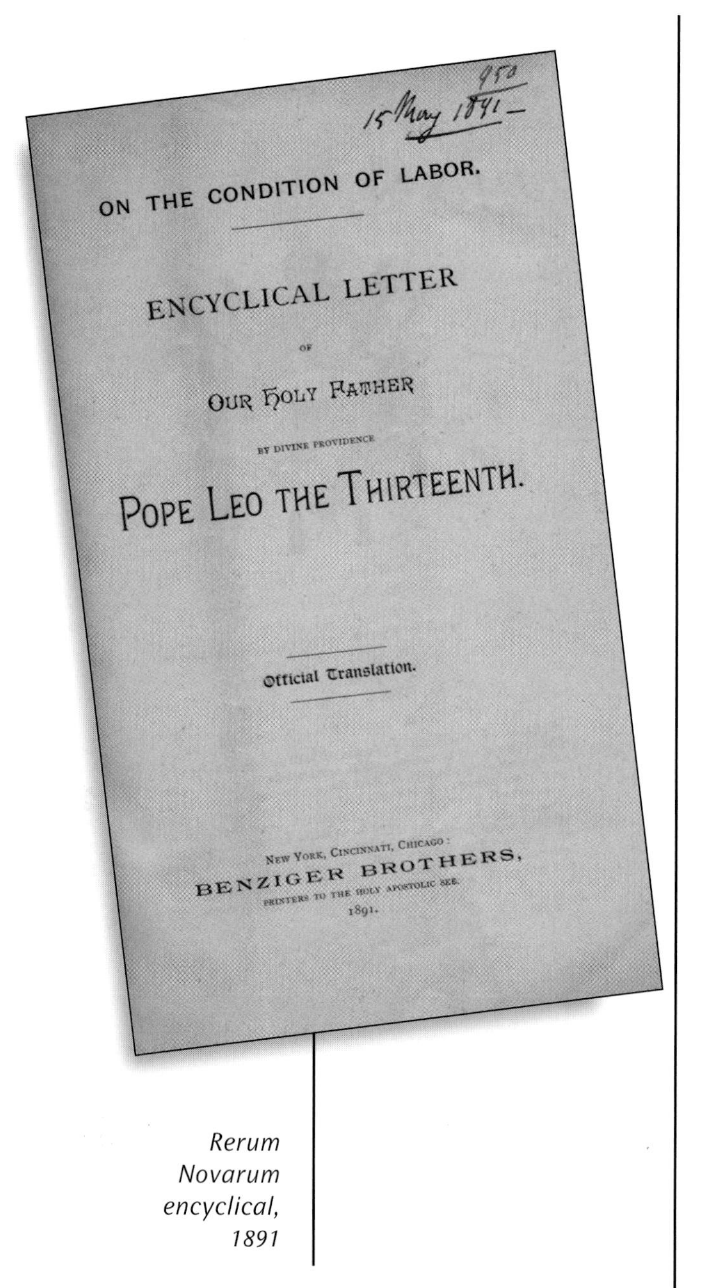
ON THE CONDITION OF LABOR.

ENCYCLICAL LETTER

OF

OUR HOLY FATHER

BY DIVINE PROVIDENCE

POPE LEO THE THIRTEENTH.

Official Translation.

NEW YORK, CINCINNATI, CHICAGO:
BENZIGER BROTHERS,
PRINTERS TO THE HOLY APOSTOLIC SEE.
1891.

Rerum Novarum encyclical, 1891

The years between the end of World War I and the Great Depression were a time of intensified social turmoil and conflict in the Pacific Northwest. The region experienced a wave of strikes as the International Workers of the World (IWW), Bolsheviks, and socialist organizers mobilized laboring men and women as part of their efforts to secure better wages and working conditions and to reform economic and social arrangements in society.

The majority of labor organizers and large numbers of working people, drawing on lessons from Europe's past, viewed the Roman Catholic Church as an ally of those economic and political forces whose interest was to keep laboring people working for low wages and no benefits. In Seattle, O'Dea felt the sting of their attacks. Against the "atheistic" socialism of the IWW and others, O'Dea promoted Leo XIII's encyclical "*Rerum Novarum.*" The *Progress* called it the "Magna Carta of the working man." The encyclical was referenced whenever laboring rights were threatened, in Labor Day editorials, and subsequently, whenever right-to-work laws were proposed.

A set of issues converged in the 1920s to create multiple challenges for O'Dea and the Catholic Church. The Church had the task of publicizing its approach to the problems of labor and helping working people discriminate between papal and socialist approaches. The Church was in the minority on the issue of prohibition; Catholics were separated politically from social progressives on the issue of parochial schools; and finally, the Church's defense of new immigrants put it at odds with both progressives and super-patriots who saw the newcomers as a threat to the American way of life. The convergence of all these forces made the 1920s an awkward time during which isolation and defensiveness characterized much of Catholic life in the United States.

Following World War I, nativist activities multiplied in the Pacific Northwest. Japanese nationals were threatened and harassed. In Washington, the term "foreigners" was often used to describe everyone who was not of Nordic background and Protestant. African-American/Blacks, Jews, southern Europeans (mostly Catholic), and Asians were particular targets. Racism continued to be a constant reality in the lives of African-Americans, Asians, Pacific Islanders, the few East Indians remaining after mass expulsions in 1907, and Hispanic and Latino peoples in Washington State during the 1920s.

Aware of growing numbers of Asians in his diocese, O'Dea invited the Maryknoll Fathers to Seattle to care for the Japanese. In April, 1920, Maryknoll priests became a presence in Seattle. In May, Sisters Teresa and Gemma, M.M., opened a kindergarten for Japanese children. The National Council of Catholic Men provided monetary support for the Catholic Filipino Club in Seattle. This organization supported ministry to Filipinos, especially to students who were sent to the States by the U.S. government to study and subsequently return to the Philippines.

Catholic Filipino Club, 1928

Our Lady Queen of Martyrs School with Maryknoll sisters

On September 8, 1921, church and city turned out to celebrate Edward O'Dea's silver jubilee as a bishop. Several bishops and thousands of lay people gathered to celebrate. An evening civic event attended by the governor of the state, the mayor, and other prominent citizens paid tribute to O'Dea. He was given $35,000.00 from the priests and the Knights of Columbus, with which he paid for the Bishop's residence on Spring Street in Seattle. O'Dea marked his jubilee with a surge of building projects. In the fall of 1921, he dedicated three new churches, Assumption in Bellingham, Our Lady Star of the Sea in Bremerton, and Holy Rosary in Tacoma. In 1922, a program of school construction began in Seattle that was never equaled in cities of comparative size. Nine schools were built in twelve months. By September, 1923, thirty parochial schools were in operation in parishes throughout the diocese. In 1924, O'Dea High School was dedicated.

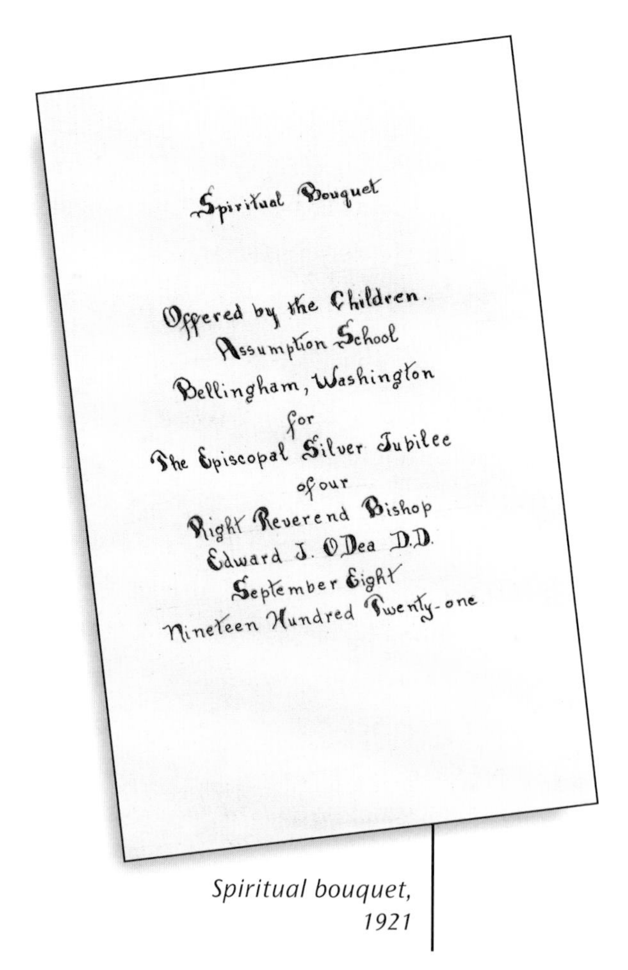

Spiritual Bouquet

Offered by the Children
Assumption School
Bellingham, Washington
for
The Episcopal Silver Jubilee
of our
Right Reverend Bishop
Edward J. O'Dea D.D.
September Eight
Nineteen Hundred Twenty-one

Spiritual bouquet, 1921

O'Dea's silver jubilee

Altar boys at O'Dea jubilee celebration

Cathedral High School, Seattle

O'Dea's building campaign was more than a celebration, however. It also embodied the importance of the Church and Catholic education to confront the challenges of the world. For O'Dea, Catholic institutions teaching eternal and timeless truths to humans caught up in a period of momentous change and disruption were vital to the survival of western civilization. The bishop's annual Christmas letter for 1921 reflected on the state of the world and the Diocese of Seattle over the preceding twenty-five years.

Christmas Greetings

Theologically speaking there is no difference between the Christmas of 1921 and that of 1896. But what momentous changes have taken place during this quarter of a century in nearly every part of the habitable globe. The recent appalling world-war and its concomitant evils have almost undermined the foundations of Christian civilization because the lessons taught by the Son of God from His crib in Bethlehem have been ignored by the majority of mankind. The narrative of His beloved disciple, "He came into His own, and His own received Him not", is as true today as it was on the first Christmas twenty centuries ago.

In the midst of this well nigh universal repudiation, Holy Mother Church has always remained true to Him and to His heavenly doctrines. Acting through her divinely appointed Head on earth, she has in season and out of season proclaimed from the house-tops the eternal principles of justice and charity. She stands out like a Gibralter stemming the ever advancing tide of socialism and political unrest. All glory, therefore, to the Church universal!

But may not the Church in the Diocese of Seattle claim some small share of this glory for her labors of nearly three quarters of a century in proclaiming the saving doctrines of Christ instilling them into the hearts and lives of men? During the last twenty five years she has made truly wonderful progress, temporal as well as spiritual, and has been a powerful factor for good in this State of Washington. In 1896 she was, we might say "in swaddling clothes and laid in a manger", but today she appears like a well developed and robust youth, proud of her achievements, of her ever increasing army of zealous and devoted priests, of her numerous religious Orders of self-sacrificing and devoted men and women, glorying in her numerous beautiful churches and magnificent institutions of learning and charity. This splendid record of twenty five years is indeed well calculated to fill our hearts with joy and gratitude to God at this season, but we cannot help lamenting the fact that in this year of Our Lord

O'Dea's Christmas Greeting, 1921

Christmas Greetings page 2

1921 the world is far from enjoying that peace which was proclaimed on the Judean hillsides two thousand years ago. And why? The Church has not failed in her divine mission, Christianity has not failed, Christ our Lord has not failed. But why is there no peace on earth? The answer is simple. "Peace on earth" depends upon "men of good will", and not upon greed nor the sordid expedients and wranglings of politicians.

Let us hope and pray that He who came to bring that peace on earth which "the world does not know" will bless the deliberations of the representatives of the nations now engaged in the peace conference in Washington, and that the peace proclaimed on the first Christmas morn will return to earth once more and abide with us all forever.

December 1921. Bishop of Seattle

In the 1920s, a resurgence of nativism led to a campaign that targeted Catholic schools in Oregon and Washington. This continued a long tradition of anti-Catholic sentiment and stories that had appeared in the United States beginning in the 1820s. These stories presented Catholics as disloyal to the country because of their religious allegiance to the pope. For example, during the campaign for the Oregon School Bill one issue of the *Klamath Falls Herald* printed that at the birth of every male child in a Catholic family, a gun and ammunition are buried underneath the church to prepare for the day that the government will be overthrown on behalf of the pope. The great Catholic menace to the United States had to be overcome by bible-believing Protestant Christians capable of independent thinking as individuals and practiced in self-control.

In Washington the nativist attack came in the form of Initiative 49, a "compulsory public education bill" modeled on the one that had passed in Oregon in 1922. The bill was the work of the Ku Klux Klan and its purpose was to outlaw parochial schools. Despite the fact that the Oregon law was declared unconstitutional by the U.S. District Court in Portland in March, 1924, the Klan campaign for Initiative 49 continued with the drive to secure signatures to place the measure on the ballot. On July 3, 1924, the initiative's backers filed Initiative 49 with the Washington State attorney general accompanied by petitions with 55,638 signatures.

The election was held on November 5, 1924. More than 131,000 voters favored the initiative, yet it was defeated by 59,000 votes. Any attempt to mount another campaign, however, was cut off when on June 1, 1925, the U.S. Supreme Court declared the Oregon School Bill unconstitutional.

Initiative 49 handbill

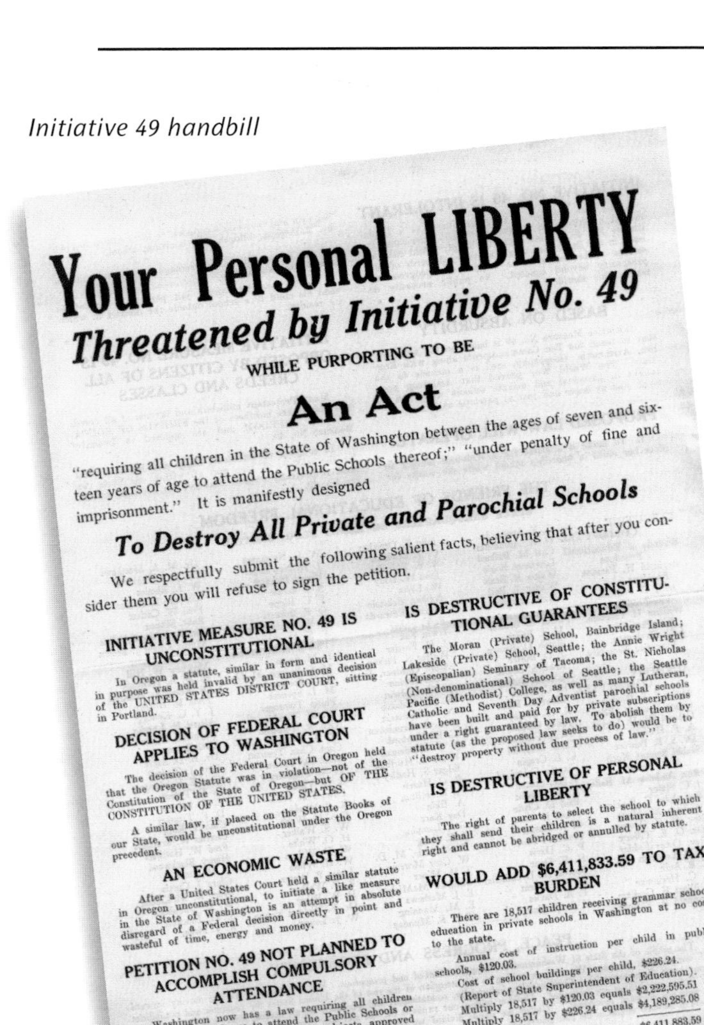

Your Personal LIBERTY

Threatened by Initiative No. 49

WHILE PURPORTING TO BE

An Act

"requiring all children in the State of Washington between the ages of seven and sixteen years of age to attend the Public Schools thereof;" "under penalty of fine and imprisonment." It is manifestly designed

To Destroy All Private and Parochial Schools

We respectfully submit the following salient facts, believing that after you consider them you will refuse to sign the petition.

INITIATIVE MEASURE NO. 49 IS UNCONSTITUTIONAL

In Oregon a statute, similar in form and identical in purpose was held invalid by an unanimous decision of the UNITED STATES DISTRICT COURT, sitting in Portland.

DECISION OF FEDERAL COURT APPLIES TO WASHINGTON

The decision of the Federal Court in Oregon held that the Oregon Statute was in violation—not of the Constitution of the State of Oregon—but OF THE CONSTITUTION OF THE UNITED STATES.

A similar law, if placed on the Statute Books of our State, would be unconstitutional under the Oregon precedent.

AN ECONOMIC WASTE

After a United States Court held a similar statute in Oregon unconstitutional, to initiate a like measure in the State of Washington is an attempt in absolute disregard of a Federal decision directly in point and wasteful of time, energy and money.

PETITION NO. 49 NOT PLANNED TO ACCOMPLISH COMPULSORY ATTENDANCE

Washington now has a law requiring all children of grammar school age to attend the Public Schools or private schools teaching equivalent subjects approved by the State. The only purpose of Initiative No. 49 is to destroy private and parochial schools. It is destructive, not constructive.

IS DESTRUCTIVE OF CONSTITUTIONAL GUARANTEES

The Moran (Private) School, Bainbridge Island; Lakeside (Private) School, Seattle; the Annie Wright (Episcopalian) Seminary of Tacoma; the St. Nicholas (Non-denominational) School of Seattle; the Seattle Pacific (Methodist) College, as well as many Lutheran, Catholic and Seventh Day Adventist parochial schools have been built and paid for by private subscriptions under a right guaranteed by law. To abolish them by statute (as the proposed law seeks to do) would be to "destroy property without due process of law."

IS DESTRUCTIVE OF PERSONAL LIBERTY

The right of parents to select the school to which they shall send their children is a natural inherent right and cannot be abridged or annulled by statute.

WOULD ADD $6,411,833.59 TO TAX BURDEN

There are 18,517 children receiving grammar school education in private schools in Washington at no cost to the state.

Annual cost of instruction per child in public schools, $120.03.

Cost of school buildings per child, $226.24.

(Report of State Superintendent of Education).

Multiply 18,517 by $120.03 equals $2,222,595.51

Multiply 18,517 by $226.24 equals $4,189,285.08

Total $6,411,883.59

The basic facts of the case make clear that anti-Catholic sentiment was strong in Washington State in the 1920s. Equally significant, however, is how the campaign against Initiative 49 was organized and carried out. The campaign was organized and led by prominent Catholic laymen. O'Dea relied on the advice of a trusted circle of prominent laymen, especially William Pigott and J.J. Donovan. Pigott chaired the Educational Committee, comprised primarily of prominent laymen from Seattle and towns throughout the diocese.

J.J. Donovan, who was at the time president of the Catholic Federated Societies in Washington, outlined in a letter to O'Dea in January of 1924 the general approach that the committee would take, focusing the campaign around the good of the community

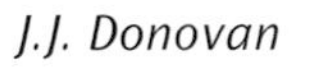

J.J. Donovan

William Pigott (right of O'Dea) and the St. James Cathedral Building Commission

and working cooperatively with non-Catholics to defeat the initiative. The Educational Committee spearheaded a campaign that focused on parishes, newspapers, government officials, labor organizations, and business leaders. Wealthy members donated funds to the campaign and used their influence to secure loans from other sources.

One prong of the campaign accelerated the Americanization process by calling for the organization of all parishes by precinct, encouraging voter registration, and calling for active participation in the anti-49 campaign on the part of all Catholic citizens. Each pastor was called upon to canvas his parish to determine the number of registered voters, and then to carry out voter-registration drives among those not yet registered. Each parish was to designate registered voters to become precinct workers and become actively involved in the political life of the precinct.

Once the initiative's petitions were submitted in Olympia, the anti-49 campaign turned to garnering votes to defeat the measure in the November election. The insistence on voter registration and participation in parishes heightened. Minutes of a meeting of representatives from parishes with the Educational Committee on October 1, 1924, show a wide disparity in the number of Catholics registered in Seattle parishes, from 95% in Holy Rosary to fewer than 50% in Our Lady of Lourdes. Automobiles were arranged to take people to the polls. Ethnic chairmen were appointed to work with particular groups of new immigrants such as Austrians and Italians.

Besides exhortation to political activism, parishes also were encouraged to pray. The bishop directed priests to add in the daily Mass the Oration "*Contra Persecutors et Male Agentes,*" and at the end of Mass the recitation of a special prayer "For Our Schools." He also directed the prayer for schools to be recited in schools "until further notice." The Educational Committee's executive secretary, William O'Connell, requested that the bishop suggest to all pastors that "all our people and especially the children of our schools . . . receive Holy Communion on Sunday, November 2, that God may give us victory" and that "we would draw mightily upon Omnipotent Power."

The Educational Committee worked behind the scenes with regard to the general public. It did not seek publicity for itself and used the authority of the bishop to direct activities in parishes.

For the general public campaign the Educational Committee cooperated closely with, and quietly helped to fund, an ecumenical organization known as the Friends of Educational Freedom. This ecumenical group of prominent businessmen, civic leaders, and Protestant religious leaders publicly opposed the initiative, speaking at gatherings and distributing literature. They described themselves as "a non-political and non-sectarian association, including public educators, business men and Protestant ministers of all denominations, organized to protect constitutional liberty, public and private schools and to promote the American spirit of tolerance and fair play." One of their handbills urged people to vote against Initiative 49 "for the sake of fair play, for harmony, for home rights."

The Friends of Educational Freedom solicited national celebrities to help with the cause. One press release even featured Babe Ruth. In all their literature, the Friends of Educational Freedom minimized the religious dimension of the initiative and accented economic self-interest and decency. Such an approach was essential if the Catholic position was to win out in a state where Catholics were a minority of the population.

Release on receipt.
Friends of Educational Freedom.

Sent to all Dailies in State

If it had not been for a private industrial school of Baltimore, Babe Ruth, the great home-run king, would probably never have been heard of. On the occasion of his recent visit to Seattle, Babe took time out to deliver his opinion on the value of private institutions.

"I understand there's a move on here in this State to knock the private schools and orphan schools for a row of pineapplies," Babe remarked. "I certainly don't think that would be a good thing to do. I was an orphan and was taken care of for fourteen years in St. Mary's Industrial School of Baltimore. That's a place where kids are given training in taking care of themselves so that they can support themselves just as soon as they are able to. Their schooling comes along with their industrial work.

"There's a lot of kids that need that training and they need to have it so they can take care of themselves. Some kids need the heavy stuff and some of them need vocational training. I don't know any other place they can get it than such a school as I went to. I know public schools don't give it."

The move the great Bambino referred to is Initiative Measure No. 49, which is designed to drive out of existence all private schools and all institutions such as orphanages with private schools in connection.

--2--

Babe Ruth press release, Friends of Educational Freedom

Another constituency important to the success of the anti-49 campaign was labor. Leaders of the anti-49 campaign in Washington talked with unions and received assistance from organizations such as the Longshoremen's Checkers Union, the International Longshoremen's Association, and the State Labor Federation.

The defeat of Initiative 49 led all involved to reflect on the campaign, its meaning, and its results. Donovan expressed clearly to O'Dea the debt Catholics in Washington owed to non-Catholics who had cooperated in the campaign, *We really should be very grateful to all the gentlemen who signed the circulars of the Friends of Educational Freedom, and especially to the Lutheran and Adventist clergy who made a gallant fight in this whole affair. . . . The Episcopalians, Congregationalists, Presbyterians, and Methodists, through their clergy and leaders have all done valiant service against the Klan and for tolerance and fair play.*

Lay, ecumenical and interethnic in character, and argued with reference to economic interests and the common good and appeals to protect American freedoms, the campaign against Initiative 49 showed how Catholics could have influence politically in Washington State, despite being a minority of the population. In the process, it exposed ordinary Catholics to the possibilities of ecumenical cooperation 40 years before Vatican II would pave the way for lay ecumenism. As well, the campaign revealed how Catholic laity who had succeeded in the U.S. for a generation would negotiate their faith and their political life on their own terms.

The participation of lay organizations in the anti-49 campaign confirmed O'Dea's knowledge that the laity were significant for the work of the Church. The bishop relied even more than in the previous decade on the Knights of Columbus, the Catholic Daughters of America, the Diocesan Council of Catholic Women and other lay organizations for resources to carry out various ministries in the diocese. Lay participants in the anti-49 campaign came away with a greater sense of their own identity and autonomy as Catholics. As lay Catholics became more prosperous, they expressed their commitment to the Church. In 1923 a Seattle layman, Frank Sullivan and his pastor at Immaculate, Father William Culligan, S.J., developed a Dollar-a-Sunday program that gained national attention.

Catholic laity continued to participate in sodalities and confraternities but different devotions came to replace them for some Catholics in the 1920s. Forty Hours Devotion, which had been popular since the 1890s, continued to attract participants. Novenas grew in popularity, especially those to the Sorrowful Mother, Our Lady of Perpetual Help, St. Jude, and the Sacred Heart. In the Diocese of Seattle, as in the rest of the United States, the 1920s saw American Catholics, many of them recent immigrants or the children of immigrants, drawn more fully into the political and economic mainstream of the nation's life, even as they continued to live quite separate religious lives.

The massive building projects Bishop O'Dea undertook in 1921 had put the diocese heavily in debt, over $1,000,000 outstanding. The campaign against Initiative 49 also proved costly. For the rest of the decade the diocese would struggle financially. Despite this burden of debt, O'Dea

Cathedral debt clock (in background)

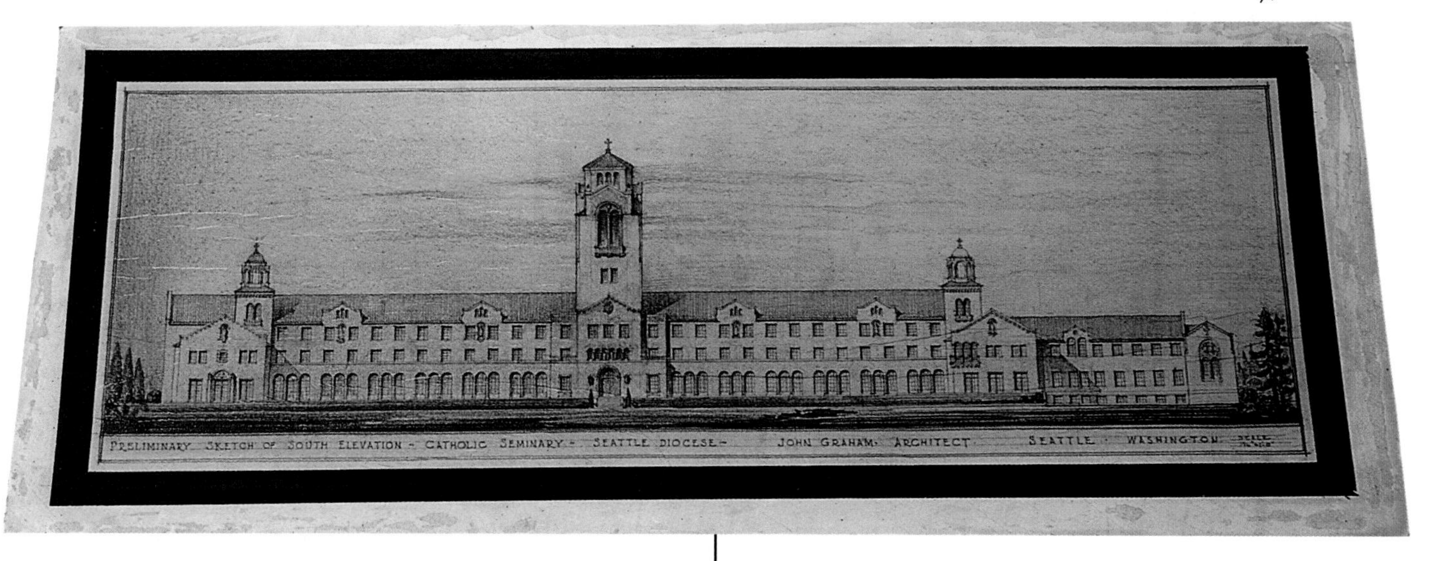

proceeded with his dream of establishing a seminary. In 1926 the bishop purchased a site on the north shore of Lake Washington and began plans for building a seminary and staffing it with priests from the Society of St. Sulpice. On October 13, 1930, the Apostolic Delegate, Archbishop Pietro Fumasoni-Biondi laid the cornerstone for St. Edward Seminary. The seminary was completed a year later and dedicated on October 13, 1931. By this time O'Dea was both aged and ill. He lived to celebrate his golden jubilee as a priest, a grand celebration held on November 24, 1932, that honored the bishop as a great builder of Catholic institutions. As Archbishop Edward Howard of Oregon City declared, *Cross crowned towers pointing to Heaven from Seattle's seven hills proclaim to every visitor, as in the eternal city, that a man of God, an apostle of Christ, has labored here and placed his stamp for all men to see.*

O'Dea stated, *I am grateful to God for the clergy, the sisters, brothers and religious of the diocese. They are my crown and my glory–grateful for all they have done to help and support me during these years. Without them, I could have done nothing.*

On Christmas night, 1932, Edward J. O'Dea died. He left his gold snuff box and his library to St. Edward Seminary.

Little Daughters of St. Joseph, St. Edward Seminary

Chapter 4

THE GREAT DEPRESSION THROUGH WORLD WAR II, 1929-1946

The rain and dark clouds that marked Bishop O'Dea's funeral day portended difficulties to come. The Depression crippled the Northwest for a decade, dominating everyday life. Many of the jobless clustered wherever they could find shelter. In Seattle, Hooverville arose, one of the largest of the homeless encampments. The region's situation was aggravated by the arrival of 200,000 or more refugees from the Dust Bowl of the Great Plains. They entered the Northwest seeking economic betterment as had the Euro-Americans, African-Americans, Hispanics, and Asian and Pacific Island peoples who arrived before them.

Hooverville, 1933

Gerald Shaughnessy, S.M.

For the Diocese of Seattle, the Depression was a nearly crushing blow. Heavy debt, a dying bishop, and increasing numbers of Catholic people and others needing help presented almost insurmountable problems. The infrastructure of institutions and voluntary associations that had emerged and grown during O'Dea's episcopacy was not sufficient to meet the need.

In July, 1933, Gerald Shaughnessy, S.M., was appointed fourth bishop of the Diocese of Seattle. Shaughnessy was born in Massachusetts in 1887. He was educated in public schools and attended Boston College. After graduation he taught in Montana, and at the Marist College in Utah. Shaughnessy entered the Society of Mary in 1916 and in 1920, at the age of 33, he was ordained. In 1925 he received a doctorate in sacred theology from Catholic University of America. In 1919, Shaughnessy had begun working in the office of the Apostolic Delegate and continued working there until his appointment to Seattle.

Most in Seattle had no idea who the new bishop was. But Monsignor Theodore Ryan, who had served as O'Dea's chancellor and secretary, knew that all Seattle matters had been handled by Shaughnessy at the Delegate's office.

Shaughnessy was consecrated on September 19, 1933, in the crypt of the National Shrine in Washington, D.C. Among the Seattle priests in attendance were two who had been present at O'Dea's consecration in 1896, Monsignors Gustave Achtergael and John Sweens. The *Catholic Northwest Progress* covered Shaughnessy's consecration, his trip west, and his arrival and installation in Seattle in detail.

The installation took place on October 10, 1933, presided over by Archbishop Howard. Shaughnessy's installation was broadcast on the radio station KOL. This was a first for Seattle and indicated the bishop's willingness to innovate—to adopt new technologies and practices that would promote the Catholic Church.

Shaughnessy was a career bureaucrat and brought to the diocese his attention to minute detail and his passion for the organization and smooth functioning of all institutions under his charge. While his style and focus required adjustment on the part of his priests, chancery staff, and laity of the diocese, it also was the resource that allowed him to bring the diocese back from the brink of financial collapse.

One challenge shared by all his predecessors was to provide priests and male and female religious to minister to the people of the diocese. He actively recruited priests from other sections of the United States and Europe. On confirmation tours he repeatedly stressed the need to cultivate

Shaughnessy at the Chancery, 1947

vocations to the priesthood and to religious life. He instituted an annual novena for vocations in the diocese.

Vocations became the focus of the Serra Club, formally organized in Seattle on February 27, 1935, by local Catholic businessmen. Junipero Serra was chosen as patron because it was a name distinctively Catholic, American, and Western. Father Serra had founded the California missions and was recognized as a significant historical figure on the Pacific Slope. As others joined the original group, it was decided that a worthwhile Catholic objective was needed. In doing so the men were practicing what had become known as Catholic Action. On June 12, 1935, the group decided that its purpose would be financial aid for young men studying for the priesthood and the fostering of religious vocations. The group was nothing if not ambitious, and on July 8, 1939, Serra International was formed at a meeting in Seattle with representatives from clubs then existing in Seattle, Spokane, Tacoma, Portland, and San Francisco.

By 1950 the movement had spread to fifty-six cities in North America and had a membership of over 4,000, and in 1951 the Pope recognized the work of the Serrans when he affiliated them with the Pontifical Work for Priestly Vocations, part of the Sacred Congregation of Seminaries and Universities.

The Serra Club also had another purpose; to foster friendships and collaboration among Catholic leaders. Serra, then, continued the kind of attention to Catholic projects, but with an eye to civic interests and the Church's status in the community, that had characterized the men who participated in the Education Committee that worked to defeat Initiative 49.

As the Depression dragged on, Shaughnessy went about stabilizing the finances of the diocese and restructuring the chancery so that diocesan programs might match the demographic realities of the region. Population size and density, and urban and industrial growth had transformed western Washington and would continue to do so, even more dramatically once World War II began. In 1933 the population of Washington was approximately 1,600,000. By the time of Shaughnessy's death in 1950 it was nearly 2,400,000, an increase of 48%.

By the mid-1930s it became clear that increasing numbers of Catholic children were not in parochial schools. Shaughnessy responded by establishing the Confraternity of Christian Doctrine (CCD) in the diocese. A nationally recognized speaker, Marian Marks, was asked to address the first assembly of priests, religious, and laity held to promote the establishment of CCD. Shaughnessy wanted the Church in Seattle to have the same stature as the Church in large eastern dioceses with much greater numbers of Catholics. Thus, he brought in or developed programs and activities that would bring recognition to the diocese.

Christmas Official, *Dec. 10, 1934*

OFFICE OF THE BISHOP

DIOCESE OF SEATTLE
907 TERRY AVENUE
SEATTLE

OFFICIAL
1934 - 12-C

December 10, 1934

TO ALL THE PASTORS IN KING COUNTY:

Reverend and dear Father:

The Washington Emergency Relief Administration, in asking my assistance in finding ten thousand $5.00 jobs for heads of families in King County between now and Christmas, has asked me to get in touch with every Pastor in the County so that the people may be informed of this $5.00 Christmas job drive. I would accordingly ask you to announce to your people that this drive for jobs is being made.

May I ask you to have those who are able to hire some of these prospective heads of families for these small jobs report to you so that you in turn may forward the names and addresses to SEneca 2761, asking for the Christmas Job Department. Of course, those who may be in a position to hire these people may telephone directly to the address given, without putting you to the bother. The actual address of the agency is: The Washington Emergency Relief Administration, Old Times Building, 410 Olive Way, Seattle.

Thanking you for your cooperation, I remain

Sincerely yours in Christ

+ Gerald Shaughnessy, S.M.

(Most Rev.) Gerald Shaughnessy, S.M.
Bishop of Seattle

SERRA CLUB HONORS LEADERS

Serra Club members of the Northwest assembled at dinner in the Gowman Hotel, Seattle, Friday evening, to hear inspiring messages from His Excellency the Most Reverend Bishop Shaughnessy, S.M., first chaplain of Serra International and James H. Gavin, (left) president of Serra International.

The Serra Club movement, now spreading throughout North America and reaching into South America, was inaugurated here in 1935. It has for its purpose the fostering of priestly vocations and aiding financially in the education of Seminarians.

Taking bows at the dinner meeting were the four men who started the first club, Dan Rooney, past president of Serra International, Dick Ward, Leo Sharkey and Hab Haberle.

Serra Club members and their wives came from Victoria, B. C., Portland, Tacoma, Everett and Yakima to attend the dinner. In charge of arrangements were Charles N. Smith and Rhoady Lee, proprietor of The Gowman. Jim Keefe, vice-president of Seattle Serra Club was toastmaster.

Serra Club article,
Catholic Northwest Progress

+

Nov. 22.

Dear Bishop Shaughnessy —

We are deeply grateful to you for your great generosity to us and beg God to bless you. With all the calls the Bishops have upon them, not only for this country but for all over the world, it makes us feel very humble that we who do so little get such help.

Our friends that make up our old group in Seattle keep in touch with us and two of them even visited us this summer.

Gratefully in Christ
Dorothy Day

Letter from Dorothy Day,
Nov. 22, 1946

—Official—

Place Asked For Homeless Boys

IT IS the practice of the Juvenile Court to commit to the custody of the Society of St. Vincent de Paul, Catholic boys who are homeless, or must be removed from their natural homes. These boys are not criminals or delinquents, but are in danger of becoming such through improper associations or lack of parental care.

The Society places all of these boys who do not need institutional care in homes where they perform such tasks as are suited to their age and strength in return for their board and care. Because of the number of such boys now under its supervision, the Society finds it increasingly difficult to provide satisfactory Catholic homes for them.

We appeal to our Catholic people, especially to those who are childless and the comfortably fixed financially, and we urge them to open their hearts and their homes to these little ones of God's flock. If you are able to take one or more of these boys into your home, we ask you to communicate with the Society of St. Vincent de Paul, either through your pastor, or directly at its office in the Railway Exchange Building.

By order of the Most Reverend Bishop,

THE CHANCERY OFFICE

Official announcement to be made in all Parish Churches and Missions in King County at all Masses on Sunday, October 27. Pastors are kindly requested to explain this announcement to their flock and to use every effort to locate foster homes of the type indicated.

Official,
homelessness,
Nov. 25, 1935

The bishop's bureaucratic and organizational skills proved an asset in the area of social welfare. Service to the poor and needy was carried out primarily in parishes and through lay organizations such as the St. Vincent de Paul Societies. Shaughnessy established Catholic Charities as a diocesan agency and brought in Father William Walsh from Scranton to organize the department. Walsh arrived in the diocese in January, 1936. In August of that year the National Conference of Catholic Charities held its 22nd annual meeting in Seattle. Governor Clarence Martin and Seattle's mayor, Fred Dore, addressed an audience that included two archbishops, twelve bishops and 10,000 priests, religious, and laity, describing the extent of poverty and want in the region in the midst of the Great Depression.

In 1939, Father Thomas Gill became director of Catholic Charities of the Diocese of Seattle. Catholic Charities helped to coordinate the work of orphanages, homes for the aged, and homes for troubled girls and boys. The goal of Catholic Charities was the delivery of the most efficient and effective social services possible with the available resources. The legal incorporation of Catholic Charities of the Diocese of Seattle in 1940 allowed the agency to gain access to federal funds that became increasingly available during the Depression and especially after World War II for providing social services.

Thomas Gill, director of Catholic Charities

The Society of St. Vincent de Paul continued its work through the 1930s, visiting poor families, providing food, clothing, furnishings, rent money, furniture, and heating fuel, covering hospital costs, and placing children in Catholic schools where the Society handled tuition and book expenses. Much of the money for these charitable works was generated by the Salvage Bureau, whose leader, Peter Emt, was a fixture in Seattle for thirty years. Members of the organization also held baskets at the back of churches after Sunday Mass to collect money.

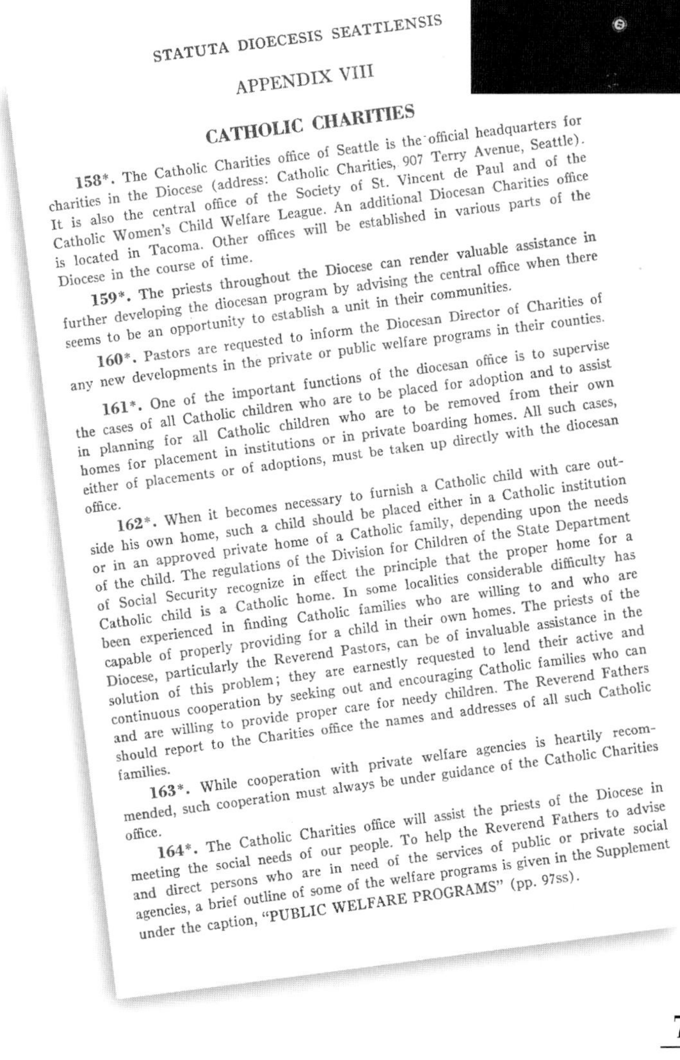

STATUTA DIOECESIS SEATTLENSIS

APPENDIX VIII

CATHOLIC CHARITIES

158*. The Catholic Charities office of Seattle is the official headquarters for charities in the Diocese (address: Catholic Charities, 907 Terry Avenue, Seattle). It is also the central office of the Society of St. Vincent de Paul and of the Catholic Women's Child Welfare League. An additional Diocesan Charities office is located in Tacoma. Other offices will be established in various parts of the Diocese in the course of time.

159*. The priests throughout the Diocese can render valuable assistance in further developing the diocesan program by advising the central office when there seems to be an opportunity to establish a unit in their communities.

160*. Pastors are requested to inform the Diocesan Director of Charities of any new developments in the private or public welfare programs in their counties.

161*. One of the important functions of the diocesan office is to supervise the cases of all Catholic children who are to be placed for adoption and to assist in planning for all Catholic children who are to be removed from their own homes for placement in institutions or in private boarding homes. All such cases, either of placements or of adoptions, must be taken up directly with the diocesan office.

162*. When it becomes necessary to furnish a Catholic child with care outside his own home, such a child should be placed either in a Catholic institution or in an approved private home of a Catholic family, depending upon the needs of the child. The regulations of the Division for Children of the State Department of Social Security recognize in effect the principle that the proper home for a Catholic child is a Catholic home. In some localities considerable difficulty has been experienced in finding Catholic families who are willing to and who are capable of properly providing for a child in their own homes. The priests of the Diocese, particularly the Reverend Pastors, can be of invaluable assistance in the solution of this problem; they are earnestly requested to lend their active and continuous cooperation by seeking out and encouraging Catholic families who can and are willing to provide proper care for needy children. The Reverend Fathers should report to the Charities office the names and addresses of all such Catholic families.

163*. While cooperation with private welfare agencies is heartily recommended, such cooperation must always be under guidance of the Catholic Charities office.

164*. The Catholic Charities office will assist the priests of the Diocese in meeting the social needs of our people. To help the Reverend Fathers to advise and direct persons who are in need of the services of public or private social agencies, a brief outline of some of the welfare programs is given in the Supplement under the caption, "PUBLIC WELFARE PROGRAMS" (pp. 97ss).

Diocesan Synodal Statutes, Catholic Charities, 1938

St. Vincent de Paul Salvage Bureau, Lake Union

Peter Emt, director, St. Vincent de Paul Salvage Bureau

Diocesan Motor Mission

Bishop Shaughnessy found ways to carry out evangelistic and educational work despite limited resources. In August, 1936, he brought a noted lay street preacher from the east to Seattle. Theodore Dorsey made his debut in Volunteer Park, engaging in "open air" polemics. He used a car equipped with an amplifier so he would not be missed. Dorsey moved to Seattle's Skid Row where he spoke on street corners as the Salvation Army preachers did, but without a brass band.

In 1937 Shaughnessy acquired a shiny trailer chapel, which was hitched to the bumper of a car. He blessed it in July, under the patronage of St. Paul, and sent it out to rural areas under the

Swinomish Indian Tribe Community, 1938

supervision of Father Joseph Gustafson of St. Edward Seminary. The first Mass in the Motor Chapel was held at Attanum Creek in Eastern Washington, site of the Oblates' old St. Joseph's Mission. That event turned the bishop's attention to the Catholic Native Americans. Though the Jesuits cared for the Yakima at White Swan, west of the Cascades there were over 2,000 Native Americans for whom little had been done since Father Boulet had left them in 1871. Shaughnessy requested that the Benedictines at St. Martin's provide them pastoral assistance. Benedict Schweitzer, O.S.B. served as missionary with residence at Port Angeles from 1938 until 1944.

During the 1930s, the Maryknoll mission continued its work with Japanese and Filipinos in Seattle. This mission had been founded in 1920 but its genesis lay in plans first proposed in 1916 by a nucleus of Seattle Japanese Catholics. The group that met with Bishop Edward O'Dea at the home of Peter Kondo and his wife Angela, included the Kondos, who had converted to Catholicism in Japan, three immigrants interested but not yet Catholic, and Messrs. Akashi and Hirata, two Catholics who traced their Catholicism back to the Japanese Martyrs of the 16th and 17th centuries. By 1925, Our Lady

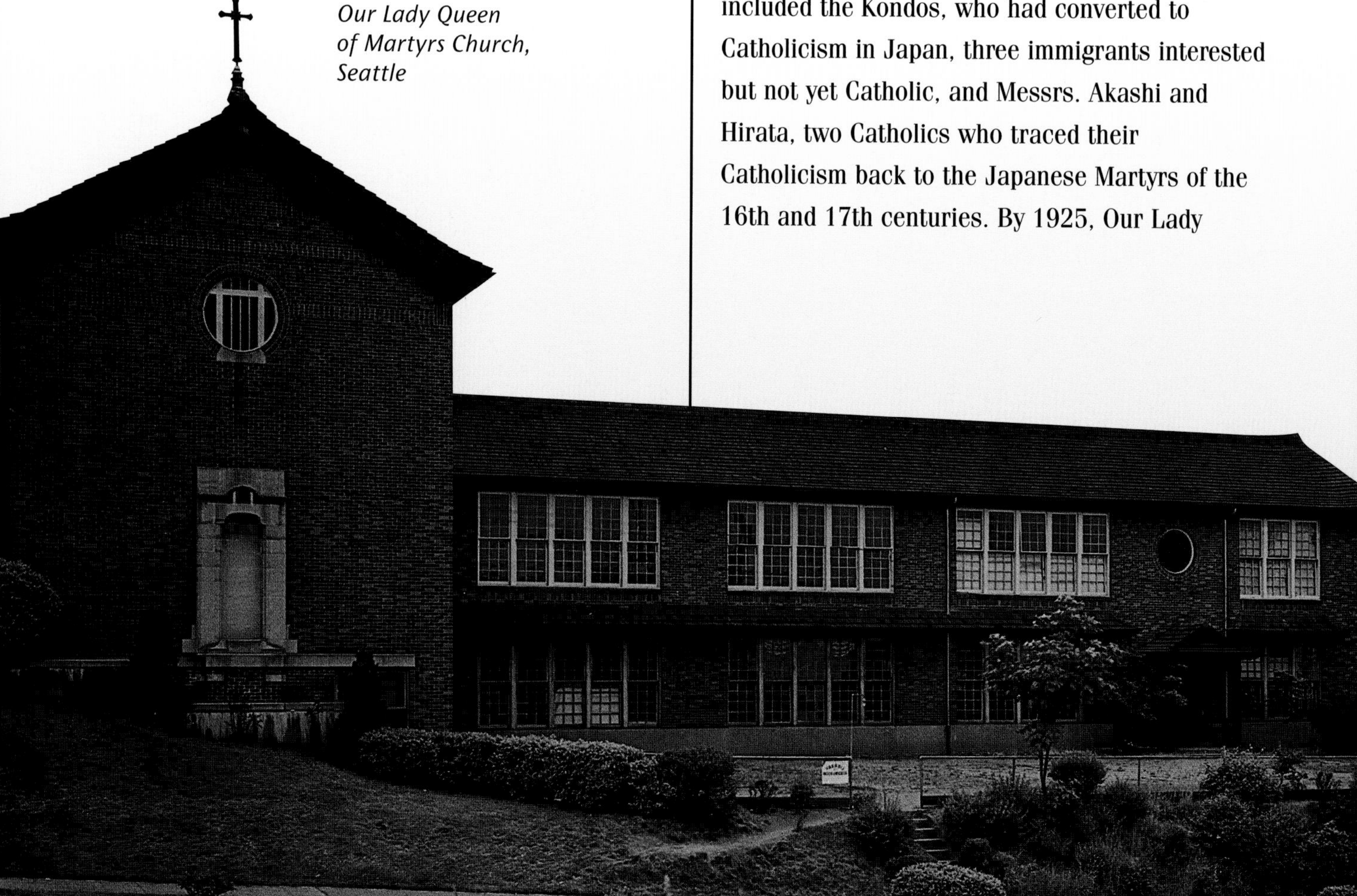

Our Lady Queen of Martyrs Church, Seattle

Queen of Martyrs became a national parish that combined Japanese and Filipino immigrants. Demographics and financial economy suggested combining the two groups in a single ministerial enterprise. In 1930, ground was broken for a Church sanctuary and social hall complex. Besides the combined Filipino/Japanese kindergarten, nursery, parochial school, weekday Mass and Sunday Mass, there was an orphanage, an employment and information bureau, a "home for old people" and a boarding house that cared for Japanese and Filipino male workers who were out of work and away from home.

This work was advanced further when, in 1935, Leopold H. Tibesar, M.M., became pastor at Our Lady Queen of Martyrs, a post he held for eleven years. Tibesar's mission strategy involved three parts. He attracted non-Catholics to the school and its programs. He tried to catechize and convert the entire family in homes where at least one member was already Catholic. Finally, he marked out for special attention key leaders in the community who showed an interest in the Church.

Tibesar promoted devotion to the Japanese Martyrs at Our Lady Queen of Martyrs. He encouraged Filipino and Japanese members of the parish to discover their common history through pageants, plays, and feast days and with symbolic recitations on radio, in homilies, and newspaper articles of the narrative of the Japanese Martyrs. The people learned the history of the evangelization of Japan and the role that Filipino Christians played in it. They also learned that after the persecution of Christians in Japan, many had left Japan for the Philippines where they assumed Filipino names and were lost to history. Tibesar saw that the story of the Japanese Martyrs was pertinent to the life of the Filipino and Japanese in Seattle, and provided a model of perseverance for Seattle's Asian Pacific Catholics. The presence of relics of the Japanese Martyrs in the church strengthened memory and provided physical connection.

In 1939, Tibesar was joined by Father Peter Monleon, a native of Boac, Marinduque, and the first priest to be ordained from his island in the Philippines. Bishop Shaughnessy and Monleon had attended graduate school together at Catholic University and Shaughnessy knew of Monleon's experience working with youth in the Philippines.

Christmas greetings to the Filipino community, 1939

OUR LADY
QUEEN OF MARTYR'S CHURCH
1603 EAST JEFFERSON ST.
SEATTLE, WASH.

To You and All Our Filipino Friends:

In the spirit of the season, we are extending our Christmas and New Year's Greetings to you hoping that the Divine Infant may shower upon you His choicest blessings.

We are offering a new schedule of Mass, in this Church, beginning Sunday, Dec. 17, 1939, at 10:30 a. m., exclusively for the Filipino Community, which will be enhanced by the singing of our special Filipino Choir.

Sincerely yours in Christ,

Rev. Leopold H. Tibesar, M. M.
Rev. Peter O. Monleon

The vibrant ministry that Tibesar and Monleon, and the Maryknoll Sisters carried out at Our Lady Queen of Martyrs was unique in its day for its multiculturalism. This ministry was enabled by an emphasis on devotional Catholicism focused around the Japanese Martyrs and the historical events of centuries earlier that created Catholic unity between the Japanese and Filipinos.

The bombing of Pearl Harbor in December of 1941 brought an end to this thriving multicultural ministry. In March of 1942, the order came to evacuate all citizens and aliens of Japanese ancestry away from the restricted military zones on the West Coast to internment camps in remote interior locations. Without the Japanese presence, the school at Our Lady Queen of Martyrs closed and parish life changed dramatically.

When the evacuation order came, the *Catholic Northwest Progress* asked: "Is this America? If it must be done, it should be with Christian charity and democratic humanity, not in the manner of a Communist tyrant...." The *Progress* also covered the continuing story of Tibesar who refused to leave his flock and traveled with them into the relocation centers and the camps.

Shaughnessy was one of the few Roman Catholic bishops in the western United States who forcefully and publicly spoke against hatred of the Japanese and unjust treatment of Japanese families. When the war ended Shaughnessy both hosted and employed the Kinoshita family when they returned to Seattle in January, 1945. The Kinoshitas were not merely the first Japanese family to arrive in Seattle, they were upstanding Catholics, members of Our Lady Queen of Martyrs, and a Gold Star family whose son and brother Francis died fighting in France in 1944. In a speech welcoming the Kinoshitas, Shaughnessy accented their American and Christian heritage: *Our welcome is extended in the true spirit of the bond of Christian, of Catholic faith which teaches us the words of Christ: 'Thou shalt love thy neighbor as thyself.' We extend an American welcome to an American family ....*

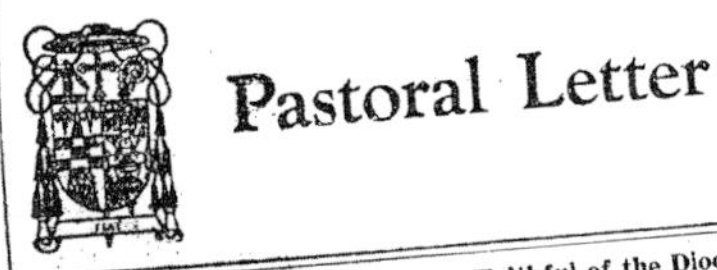

Official

Pastoral Letter

To the Clergy, the Religious and the Faithful of the Diocese, Health and Benediction in Our Lord:

IN the inscrutable designs of Providence, Almighty God has permitted events so to shape themselves that our beloved country has become engulfed in war. It is, then, the will of God that with courageous loyalty and in a spirit of patriotic sacrifice we of America shall now dedicate ourselves to the task that lies ahead. Proud of the fact that some one-third of the men in service are Catholic, one with us through membership in the Mystical Body of Christ, the Church, let us on the home front rally unanimously to our country's cause. Let us in every way support our Government in our defense program.

Let us first pray unceasingly for the safety of our armed defenders and for their success.

Let us at the same time remember that it is our patriotic duty as citizens and as members of the Church to continue with redoubled fervor, and not to cease, our prayers that an early and a just peace under God may in His mercy be vouchsafed to us.

Let us moreover especially remember, my dearly beloved in Christ, that probably the greatest evil in war, or in its aftermath, is the vice of insensate hatred, without which much of the misery and the vileness of war could never be accomplished; without which, indeed, the contentions of nations would be peacefully resolved about an arbitration table. Hatred of one's neighbor is no less, is in fact in some aspects, a greater sin in war than in peace. The second great commandment inculcated by Our Lord, "Thou shalt love thy neighbor as thyself" (Matthew 22.39) comes home to us with even greater force now that hatred of neighbor may become quite a natural reaction if we overlook the supernatural and the field of God's grace. Again let us listen to the words of Christ: "I say to you, Love your enemies: do good to them that hate you" (Matthew 5.44). Specifically we beseech all by the merits of Christ, and in the name of His Blessed Mother, to keep free from all stain of that hatred of one's neighbor that can in such a deadly manner taint the actions of even the elect. Let us in thought and word and deed refrain at all times from anything that might increase the tension among our neighbors or bring down upon them discrimination or opprobrium because of true or fancied differences

(Continued on Page 3)

(Continued from Page 1)

of citizenship, or creed or race or color. "Judge not, that you may not be judged" (Matthew 7.1).

Our Catholic heritage especially inculcates upon us in these momentous hours that we embrace our fellow American citizens of Japanese extraction in a special bond of charity, for they who are no less loyal than others, and no less claimants of true American citizenship and of all rights thereunder, need our sympathy and our love in Christ, innocent victims, as in many cases they will be, of antipathies and unreasoning prejudices. Likewise the law-abiding Japanese citizens resident in our country we should embrace in the brotherhood of man, and in the bond of that all-inclusive love of neighbor which our Blessed Savior so often and so insistently calls to our mind.

Even as this is being written word comes that we are now at war with Germany and Italy. Towards American citizens of those racial extractions we should exercise the same principles of justice and charity.

Jesus calls us not merely to love our neighbor, but to love him as we love ourselves. Love of self has its exemplification solely through love of God and obedience to His commandments. Many will indeed wonder what God would have us do in these days when perhaps personal dangers may lurk for us above the clouds. Of St. Aloysius it is told that when asked one evening at recreation what would be his course were he to learn that he had but a few minutes to live, he replied that he would continue with his present occupation. Almighty God would indeed have us face all dangers with courage and with unqualified trust in His goodness and His mercy. By every principle of faith we, for whom every moment is a step nearer to eternity, should, therefore, through recourse to the Sacraments, through devotion to our Blessed Mother, and through faith in the mercy of our Redeemer, so live each day that calmly unafraid we shall joyfully go to meet our Maker, whether He calls us in the midst of war's alarms, or from the occupations of our leisure hours, or in some more normal course of nature. In love of God let us, in short, avoid all occasion of sin, mindful of those things that God hath prepared for them that love Him. Thus shall we look forward to the day when the consoling words of the Sacred Writer apply to us: "And I heard a great voice from the throne, saying: Behold the tabernacle of God with men, and he will dwell with them. And they shall be his people: and God himself with them shall be their God. And God shall wipe away all tears from their eyes: and death shall be no more, nor mourning, nor crying, nor sorrow shall be any more, for the former things are passed away" (Apoc. 21:3, 4).

Faithfully yours in Christ

+ Gerald Shaughnessy, S.M.

Bishop of Seattle.

Dec. 12, 1941.

This letter is to be read at all Masses in churches, missions and public oratories of the diocese on Sunday, December 14.

Shaughnessy's pastoral letter, Christmas 1941

The Kinoshita family and Leopold Tibesar, M.M, at Camp Minidoka, 1945

Quickly after war was declared Shaughnessy opened the National Catholic Community Service Club in Seattle. Its purpose was to "aid and serve men who are in the service of the United States. It represents in a special way cooperation with our government in its defense." The diocese and parishes cooperated in the war effort, curtailing building projects, adjusting the times of liturgical services to comply with dim-out requirements, promoting prayer and support of the troops.

United Service Organizations-National Catholic Community Service, Oak Harbor

Catholic Seamen's Club open house

World War II brought tens of thousands of people into the diocese, both soldiers and workers. Among those who came were large numbers of African-American/Blacks. The labor shortage generated by the war provided African-American/Blacks access to industrial and clerical jobs which previously had been closed to them.

Among the African-American/Blacks who came to the Pacific Northwest were families from Louisiana with centuries-long histories as Catholics. Individuals like Emmet Pitre, who was stationed at Fort Lewis during the War, and subsequently his brothers, Clayton and John, brought a strong and active Catholicism with them. They would continue that tradition not only in the Diocese of Seattle but nationally. Clayton Pitre provided major leadership in the establishment of the Martin Luther King Jr. Daycare Center in the 1960s. Walter Hubbard served as president of the Seattle Black Catholic Lay Caucus.

In reflecting on his arrival in Seattle, Clayton Pitre described how he arrived in March, 1946. He attended St. Mary Church the first Sunday after his arrival and was amazed at how crowded it was. He wandered among Seattle parishes for seven years and sang with the Asian choir at the Maryknoll mission. He attended Seattle University and in 1952 began working as a civil servant with the federal government. That same year he purchased a house in St. Mary Parish. Pitre described how being in the military influenced his life. When he was leaving the army a chaplain said: "Go home. Take part in community life. Vote. Have an influence."
"I took that and my discharge," said Pitre.

Pitre family, Christmas 1960.
Clayton Pitre standing, holding child

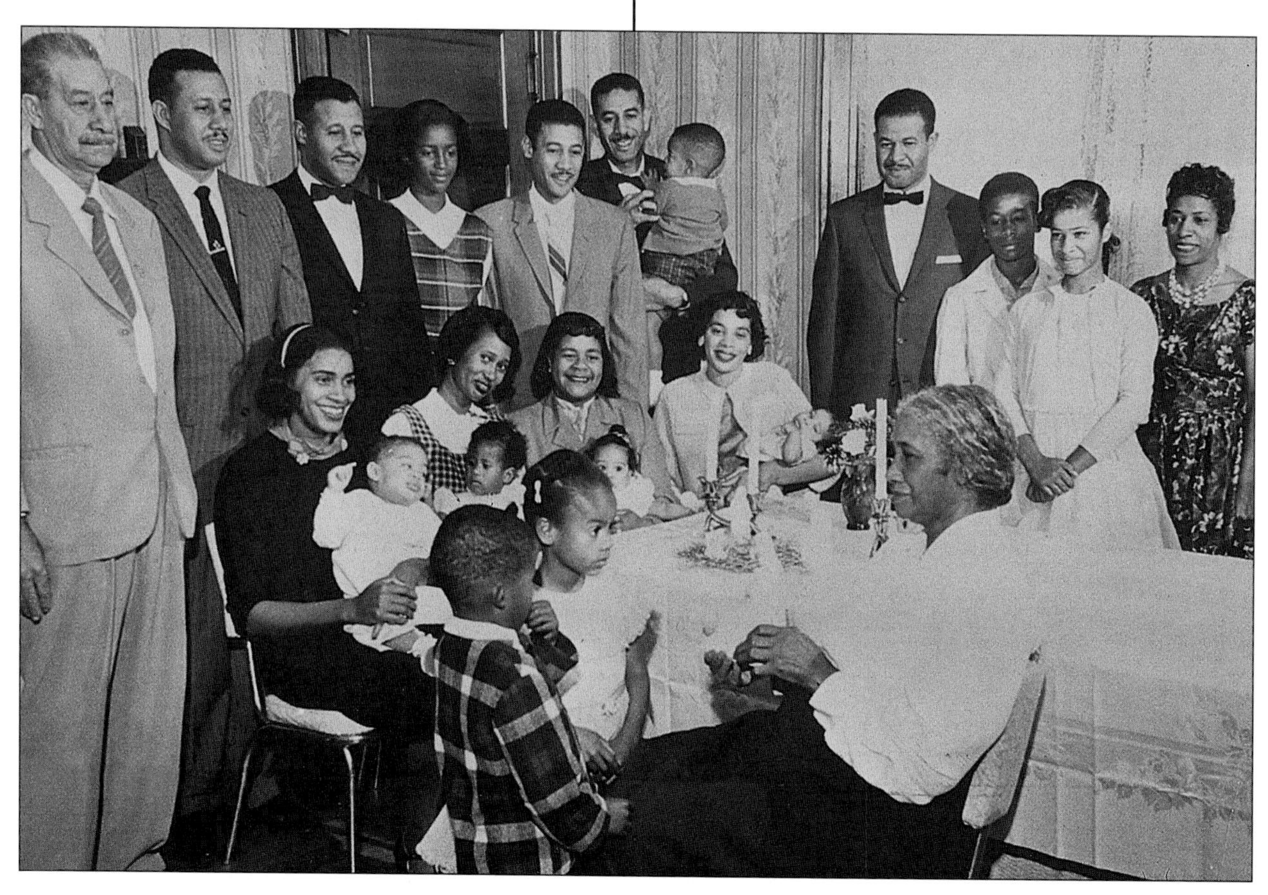

Establishment of the Martin Luther King Jr. Daycare Center. Claggett Pruett (l), Cornelius Power (seated), standing in back (l-r) Carlton Phillips, John Doherty, D. Harvey McIntyre, Walter Hubbard, John Peluso, and Dennis Muehe

Pitre became active in St. Mary Parish where he watched how evangelization worked through the parochial school in the 1960s and 1970s. He volunteered at the school and sponsored some of the children for baptism. The closing of the school in the 1970s was a severe blow to the community and led to a down-turn in the parish. Pitre was the second parish council president at St. Mary's. He worked with parishioners who were uncomfortable with having a parish council. When Hispanics began attending St. Mary's and a priest was assigned as parochial administrator instead of pastor, Pitre worked to develop connections between the African-American/Black and Hispanic communities, especially by helping the latter find a connection to the history of the community. He counts as one of his accomplishments as parish council president that when he completed his term, there was a single, unified parish council at St. Mary's.

During the war years and after, Catholics continued to live out their faith through liturgy, devotions, and celebrations. Many of these were ethnic. For example, some of the Filipino celebrations were Rizal Day, an occasion for a large procession and festival, and *Flores de Mayo* was celebrated as flowers were offered to the Blessed Mother. On Christmas Eve, a couple dressed as Mary and Joseph would lead a procession from house to house, seeking shelter on the way to Midnight Mass. The community also celebrated *Simbang Gabi*, a series of Masses held at dawn during the eight days prior to Christmas. Other ethnic groups also had distinctive feasts and celebrations.

By 1945, Shaughnessy's campaign to put the diocese back on strong financial footing was complete. The debt had been significantly reduced. Procedures were in place that would ensure fiscal responsibility. In November of that year, returning from the annual meeting of the American Bishops at Washington, D.C., Shaughnessy suffered a serious cerebral hemorrhage. He never fully recovered from this incident and after several years of enforced inactivity, died suddenly at his home on May 18, 1950.

Statue of St. Joseph

Junior Third Order of St. Francis reception, St. James Cathedral

Bishop Shaughnessy's debilitating stroke left him unable to carry on the vigorous leadership that had been his trademark. The end of World War II brought even more change to the region with the shift to a peace-time economy and the settlement of many soldiers and civilian workers who decided to remain in the region after their discharge. Once the war was over the Cold War began. Catholics would enter nearly two decades devoted to fighting godless communism and praying for peace—decades focused devotionally around Mary.

Statue of Our Lady of Lourdes

But even as recitation of the rosary and devotions to Mary became more popular, other impulses in the church were rising, for better theological education, historical understanding of the church and its liturgy, and study of scripture. In the post-war years threads of an immigrant, devotionalist Catholicism would intersect with threads of an Americanized, educated, suburban Catholicism and set the context for Vatican II.

Rosary

Finger rosary

Dome of the Assumption at Immaculate Conception Parish, Seattle

Tapestry of Our Lady of Guadalupe

Chapter 5

RETURN TO NORMALCY AND CHURCH RENEWAL

1946 - 1962

In 1948, Pope Pius XII appointed Thomas A. Connolly coadjutor bishop of Seattle with right of succession. At the time, Connolly was an auxiliary bishop in the Archdiocese of San Francisco and pastor of Mission Dolores. He was born in San Francisco in 1899, and raised in the city. He studied for the priesthood at St. Patrick's Seminary, Menlo Park, California and was ordained on June 11, 1926, by Edward J. Hanna, Archbishop of San Francisco. He went on to study canon law at Catholic University of America and work at the chancery in San Francisco.

Thomas A. Connolly

Connolly traveled to Seattle by train, greeted at each stop by the people of his diocese. In Seattle, clergy and laity welcomed him warmly. His formal installation at St. James Cathedral on April 21, 1948, saw the church filled to capacity with hundreds waiting outside for a glimpse of the bishop. The reception at the Seattle Civic Auditorium was attended by dignitaries from political, economic, and civic life. Throngs of

Connolly's arrival in Vancouver

people waited outside the auditorium, which was filled to its capacity of 6,000. Coming as he did at the end of World War II, Connolly symbolized a new beginning to the people of the Diocese of Seattle, a strong leader rooted in a faith that they could trust as they sought to make their lives normal again. The war had changed the geographic and social landscape of the Pacific Northwest. The growth in population occasioned by the war did not cease once it was over. As Connolly saw it, the region was a place to build something great. During the ceremonies, he stated: "As the great Northwest grows and expands, so will progress, step by step, the Catholic Diocese of Seattle."

Connolly quickly began to attend to the work that had accumulated during Shaughnessy's illness. Waiting were parish proposals for expansion, new schools, church renovations, new convents, and parish halls. Fiscally astute, Connolly arranged financing for the building boom that characterized the Church and the entire nation after World War II. One of Connolly's earliest projects was the renovation of the interior of St. James Cathedral and a remodeling of the rectory.

St. James Cathedral after 1950 renovation

He attended to the latter project first, turning the cathedral rectory into the most spacious residence for parish priests on the West Coast. The bishop linked the cathedral remodeling project to the celebration of the centenary of the diocese in 1950.

The centennial year of the establishment of the Diocese of Seattle was celebrated with a diocesan-wide mission crusade during Lent. Over forty mission preachers were invited to take part in the campaign. They preached missions in all of the parish churches and most of the mission chapels. The purpose of the crusade was to intensify the faith of the people in a spirit of thanksgiving for the many favors received from God and to bring home to them the urgent Holy Year appeal of Pope Pius XII for penance, pardon, and peace. The themes for the Holy Year reminded American Catholics that not all was well in the early days of the Cold War. During the summer of 1950 Connolly led a pilgrimage of priests and faithful to Rome to unite the diocesan jubilee with the Holy Year celebration of the Universal Church.

In the midst of the centenary celebrations, Gerald Shaughnessy died. With the cathedral renovation not yet complete, his funeral was held in the Church of the Immaculate Conception. Connolly automatically became the fifth bishop of Seattle.

Mission crusade article, the Catholic Northwest Progress, *1950*

MILLION INVITED TO MISSIONS

Great Crowds Attend Holy Year Mission

Great throngs, overflowing many of the churches, are attending the Holy Year missions being held throughout the Diocese of Seattle.

And at the morning Masses and evening services are a goodly number who have not been inside a church for years, some who had never been in a Catholic church. For more than a million people have received warm invitations to "make the mission" not only through the public press but in personal visits from their Catholic neighbors.

More than a half million copies of the Progress' mission tabloid are being distributed by lay men and women.

At direction of His Excellency, the Most Reverend Thomas A. Connolly, Coadjutor Bishop of

Bishop Shaughnessy funeral, Immaculate Conception Church, Seattle, 1950

The centennial Mass for the diocese was celebrated in grand style in the newly refurbished St. James Cathedral. The Apostolic Delegate, Archbishop Ameleto G. Cicognani traveled to Seattle for the occasion. The thirty-two bishops in attendance formed an impressive spectacle as they processed into the cathedral, a church that now matched those of much larger eastern dioceses. The approximately 230,000 Catholics in Washington State in 1950 constituted a small number compared to the Catholic population of large eastern cities; still, the formal centenary celebrations made clear that the Diocese of Seattle was equal to its larger diocesan sisters in vigor and devotion.

The visit of the Apostolic Delegate at the centenary speeded the creation of a third diocese in Washington State. Geography, immigration, and post-war economic developments led to the creation of new diocese, despite the fact that numbers alone would not have justified it. The completion of the Grand Coulee Dam in the 1940s and the subsequent development of the Columbia Basin into farmlands marked the beginning of a new migration to over one million acres of fertile land. The area also was seeing increasing numbers of Hispanic farm workers who worked beside Anglos and American and Canadian Indians in the fields, many of whom were at least nominally Catholic. The evangelistic and pastoral challenges the Church faced in the region could not be handled effectively from Seattle.

In Seattle, Connolly and the Apostolic Delegate sat with a map of the state and determined the boundaries for the proposed new diocese which was constructed of counties then in both the Seattle and Spokane dioceses. The Diocese of Yakima was formally erected on June 23, 1951, and announced on July 18, 1951. On September 28, 1951, Connolly consecrated Joseph Dougherty, a priest who had served as Shaughnessy's chancellor, as bishop of Yakima.

Joseph Dougherty, confirmation of Mexican-American children, St. Patrick Church, Granger, 1954

Our Lady of Lourdes School, Seattle

At the same time the Diocese of Yakima was created, Seattle was raised to an Archdiocese. Yakima, Spokane, and the newly created dioceses in Alaska comprised the suffragan sees for the new ecclesiastical province. Thomas A. Connolly became the youngest archbishop in the United States.

Providing parish plants, pastoral care, schools, and CCD for the baby boom of the post-war years occupied the diocese from 1946 until the mid-1960s. Ideally Catholic children attended Catholic schools where they would be steeped in Catholic teaching and devotion and thus prepared to negotiate the larger American environment. Religious women constituted the backbone of the Catholic school system in the 1950s. As the decade began, teaching sisters outnumbered lay teachers in Catholic schools seven to one.

St. Patrick School, Tacoma

ALICIA GONZÁLEZ-CAPESTANY AND GUDELIA ALEJO

Alicia González-Capestany, came to the Archdiocese in 1962 from Cuba. She recalls: "At the time there were very few Hispanics in the Seattle Area. I remember meeting some people who I thought were Mexican and they told me they were from Spain because at the time they didn't want to tell people that they were Mexicans." The Hispanic population in the Seattle area began to grow. Not only Mexicans, but also people from Cuba, Columbia, Chile, other countries from South America, and Spain. Until Vatican II, Mass was said in Latin, but after the Council, Mass began to be in the language of the people, which in Seattle was primarily English. In 1968 or 1969, Alicia became part of a group that discussed having Mass said in Spanish. A Spanish Jesuit who was in the area was willing to say Mass in Spanish for them.

Alicia notes: "Archbishop Connolly did not support this, however, because he understood part of the church's mission to be to help all immigrants have an American heart, which to him meant speaking English. Of course, we didn't like that idea, so, we continued to pray to have Mass in Spanish. Then, when the archbishop went on vacation, Fr. McIntyre, who was pastor at Immaculate Conception and also working in the chancery, called my husband and said, 'I'll give you permission to arrange for a Spanish Mass.' So we started having a Spanish Mass at Immaculate Conception in 1968 or 1969. We had Mass there for about 2 years."

Gudelia Alejo remembers: "When I arrived in 1974, it was suggested that I go to Mass at St. Mary's. There were about 25 families from all over the Archdiocese going to St. Mary's for the Spanish Mass. They came from Mount Vernon, Tacoma, even Vancouver. The priest was Fr. (John) Doherty. He said Mass at 1 pm on Sundays. Fr. Doherty left after 2 years and we had to look for another priest. At that time I heard there was one Dominican priest, Father Garcia, at Blessed Sacrament who would say Spanish Mass. He offered us space there. So for about 3-4 years, we had Mass at Blessed Sacrament."

During its years at Blessed Sacrament Parish, the Hispanic community continued to grow. It had many activities, such as fiestas, Guadalupe celebrations, Senior Martin de Porres, the youth group, and more. But there was tension at Blessed Sacrament, and the Spanish Mass moved to St. James Cathedral. Many, such as the Cubans, did not follow the community to this Mass. With fewer people attending, Mass was offered at 6 pm, Sunday. However, the community was no longer able to hold its cycle of celebrations, St. James was a difficult space in which to hold meetings, and the people were beginning to lose their sense of community. And so, the Spanish Mass moved once again.

Alicia and Gudelia recall that "St. Mary's opened the door for us. We had had a committee of 3 or 4 that went around to different churches, looking for a church. We went to Mount Virgin, we went to St. Joseph, we went to St. Edward, and we came here. After talking to the parish council and people, we decided that the best place was St. Mary."

Alicia mentions that having an Office of Hispanic Affairs is important: "One of the reasons things are changing is that we have an office of Hispanic Affairs. When you don't have an office at the archdiocese, it's very hard to have a relationship.... They don't understand that relationship from the archbishop, to the priests and to the different churches.... So now with the office, there are a lot of archdiocesan programs, not only from one church, that helps people from different churches do things together."

The St. Mary Parish community attempts to minister to all the different ethnic groups and to respond to their distinct needs. Gudelia points out that "...yesterday we celebrated the feast of the patroness of Columbia. We will celebrate patroness of El Salvador and of Cuba, Our Lady of Charity. In October we celebrate the feast of the patroness of Peru; in November, Our Lady of Guadalupe; in December, Posada." Catechesis is also very important. Gudelia states that the "the parish catechists give the classes for the children and on the same day for the parents. Both are learning more about the meaning of the faith, Eucharist, and first Communion. Training for confirmation is the same way. If they make commitment, they can come to the classes. Then they make commitments to learn what will be their ministry in the church. They renew their baptism during the Mass and make their commitment seriously for one year to be involved in the church. ... That is the kind of training we do. We focus on the entire family."

Alicia and Gudelia clearly state that for Hispanic people being Catholic is being Hispanic. "The culture and faith are really related for us.... That is why we need really good catechesis, so we can pass our faith into the future." Looking back on their experience at St. Mary's, they say the parish has been a blessing. They note that there were difficulties, but as Gudelia declares, "Now it is time to be brothers and sisters in doing things together. When we have bilingual liturgy we really enjoy it. Everybody in the church does. Finally we are celebrating as one."

St. Paul School, Seattle

The Catholic school child was socialized in three directions—faith, citizenship, and athletics. A student at a Catholic school generally belonged to a sodality, such as the Children of Mary, which introduced the child to a myriad of devotions. The schools observed all feast days and holy days with their appropriate devotions. In many schools it was the custom for the children to go to confession every first Thursday and to Mass every first Friday. During Lent they attended Mass daily.

The students were urged to be both good Catholics and good citizens. Citizenship was promoted through Catholic troops of Boy and Girl Scouts in the 1950s. Scouting became a partner of the Catholic school and parish. Sports were promoted in Catholic schools. They provided wholesome recreation, taught good habits, especially self-control, discipline, and for some sports, the ability to work cooperatively with others.

Our Lady of Perpetual Help School, Everett

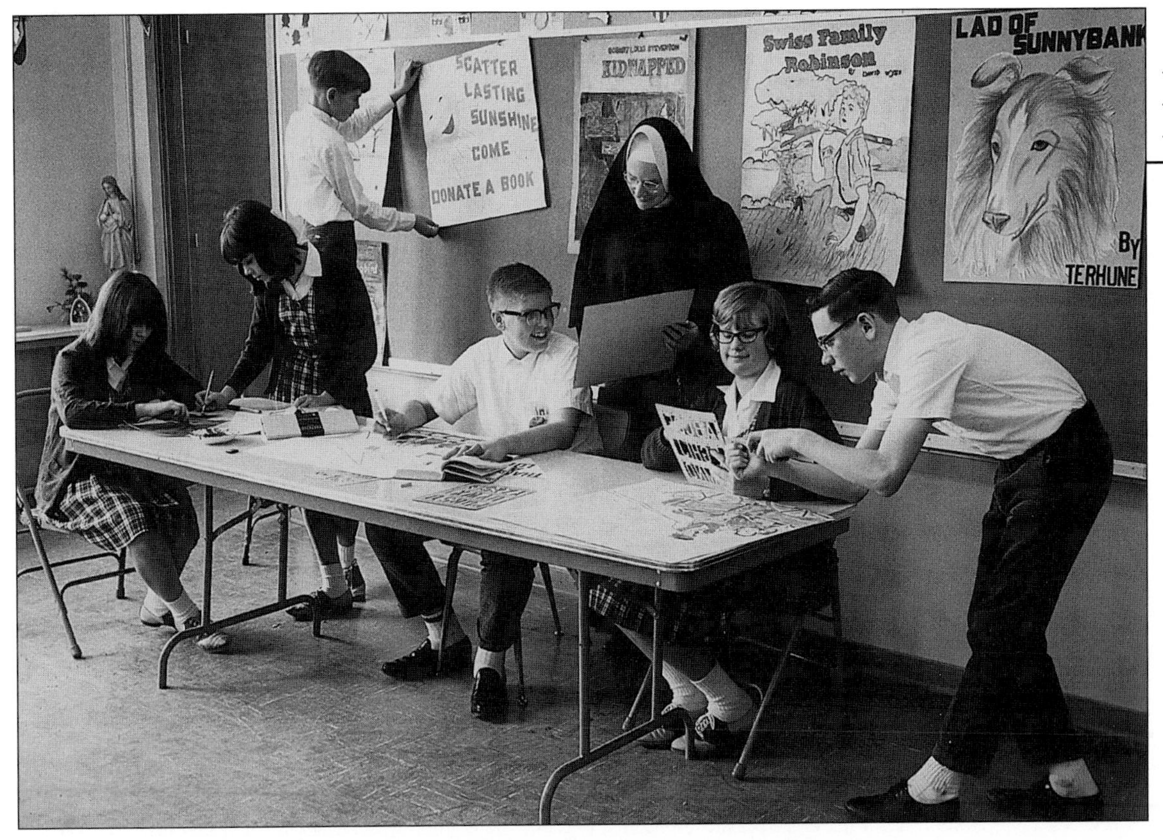

St. George School, Seattle

Boy Scouts and Archbishop Connolly, 1950

Individuals who attended Catholic schools in Seattle during the 1950s remember the time with some fondness. In a *Progress* article in the late 1980s, Gloria Rauch, a former student at St. Edward Grade School and Immaculate Conception High School in Seattle, described education as a "neater package" in the 1950s. She continued,

It was clear then what was expected and why. It was easier to be self-disciplined when the rules were set out for you.... You knew you belonged to a community, you were St. Edward's, and there were a lot of you.

Catholic high schools in the archdiocese in the 1950s were places of promise. As early as 1945 a new Catholic high school was planned. Blanchet High School in Seattle was dedicated in 1955 and in 1966, John F. Kennedy High School in Burien opened. Monsignor John P. Doogan, who had been principal at Blanchet High School, was its first principal. The sports rivalries among the Catholic high schools, including O'Dea, Seattle Preparatory, Blanchet, and Kennedy, provided steady news for the *Progress*.

John F. Kennedy High School construction, 1966

Aquinas Academy, Tacoma

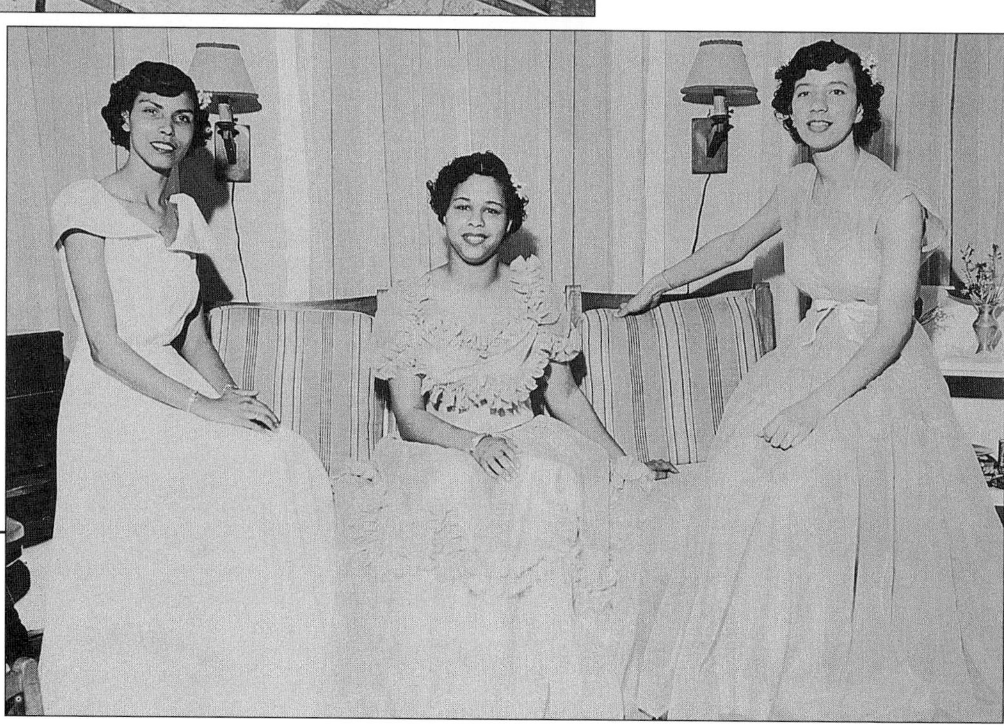

First African-American graduates from Holy Names Academy, Seattle, 1950

Blanchet High School, Seattle

When parish schools could not meet the demand and as increasing numbers of Catholic students attended public schools, catechism classes were taught weekly or biweekly. Lay catechists outnumbered women religious in Confraternity of Christian Doctrine (CCD) programs. Some parishes maintained highly effective CCD programs, others less so. In all parishes, however, participation in CCD was high during years of preparation for sacraments, first confession, first Communion, and confirmation.

Another dimension of CCD was Summer Vacation School. This religious education program was a Chautauqua for children. In smaller towns and rural parishes it was a huge success. Communities were flooded with nuns and seminarians for two weeks of concentrated study and fun, including games and magic

CCD Is The Choicest Form Of Catholic Action

CATHOLIC ACTION, if it is to be practical, must have a definite program. The Confraternity of Christian Doctrine has just such a planned campaign. It gives everyone a chance to take part in the primary work of the Church—preaching the Gospel to every creature

ADVANCE GUARD is the Home Visitor corps—the Fishers. They find those who need instruction and turn them over to the

TEACHERS, who explain the mysteries of faith. They receive valuable assistance, material and financial if needed, from the

HELPERS, who supply necessary equipment for the work. These three groups labor especially so that children who are deprived of a Catholic education will not be denied the

OPPORTUNITY of knowing their precious heritage of faith. In vacation and school-year religion classes these young people learn the

LOVE OF GOD AND NEIGHBOR, which is the aim of all religious

INSTRUCTION. Advanced catechetical knowledge is made available to high school youth and adults through

CLUBS FOR DISCUSSION. This method has been proved by experience the easiest form of adult instruction, and it develops what is the Catholic layman's greatest need today—an experience in speaking about religion before others.

ASSOCIATE MEMBERSHIP permits the sick and the aged to enjoy the spiritual benefits of the Confraternity even though they cannot take active part.

CLUBS FOR PARENTS enable them to learn how best to fulfill their duties and to make

THEIR HOMES the first and most important school of religion, which it should be. Various

INDULGENCES and other spiritual privileges are available to all who are Confraternity members.

OBJECTIONS to and questions about our faith are answered and outsiders are invited to seek and learn about the true Church through the Apostolate to

NON-CATHOLICS. This activity furnishes zealous Catholics with a definite plan of convert-making, ranging from distribution of religious literature to street preaching.

CCD ad in the Catholic Northwest Progress

shows. Often these educators stayed in the homes of parishioners. For rural and small-town Catholics, their weeks with women religious and seminarians provided at least one time during the year when they met what was considered standard for a Catholic parish, the presence of sisters.

Vacation school, Our Lady Queen of Heaven, Tacoma

St. Mary School, Anacortes

CYO billboard, 1953

CYO was another immensely popular program in the Archdiocese of Seattle during the 1950s. Gordon Hamilton, who was executive director of CYO from 1952 until the mid-1970s, referred to the 1950s as the program's "golden years." The organization sponsored one-act play festivals, speech tournaments, spelling bees, a Christmas ball, and beginning in 1954, an annual convention. Teen dances were held every Friday night at the Knights of Columbus Hall for many years in the 1950s. Parishioners supported sports teams financially and with volunteer time. Men's clubs in parishes often oversaw CYO leagues, an activity that drew men who were not attracted to devotional practices into parish life.

One of the most far-reaching and popular programs in CYO, however, was camping. The first camp in the archdiocese was Camp Blanchet, located on Leo Gallagher's property on Raft Island. Hamilton brought professional expertise to the nascent camping program and expanded it. Lay people and seminarians staffed the camps. In 1952 Camp Don Bosco opened near Carnation. It too was an overwhelming success.

The curricula of CYO camps consisted of prayer, work, education, and play, woven together to provide an intense experience in living Catholic faith. All campers attended Mass each morning and so started their day with prayer. The seminarians and lay staff set examples of what it meant to be generous Catholic adults. The campers developed their own resources, engaged in individual and group activities, and shared in the work required to handle the basic needs of such a group. The camps had no TV, no radio, no comic books. The campers and their leaders used their imaginations to provide campfire entertainment each night. The *Catholic Northwest Progress* provided extensive coverage of the camping program, down to reporting the results of boxing matches.

Gordon Hamilton (r), CYO Executive Director, 1952-1975

CYO camping reinforced identity as Catholics and generated a sense of community for its participants. Campers returned year after year with some becoming counselors for younger campers, and thus developing leadership skills and an expectation of service to the Church. Friendships developed among campers from different parishes that became important in networks of Catholic lay activity. Further, given the minority status of Catholics in Washington, the camping program provided an annual immersion into a Catholic world.

CYO camp

Camp Gallagher

The generation raised in the 1950s was the first to experience an extended adolescence where education and leisure rather than paid employment or agricultural work occupied their lives. Church leaders watched the new situation with some concern, anxious to provide supervision and appropriate forms of social interaction. Teen and young adult clubs were organized in parishes. One of their purposes was to facilitate Catholic young people to meet, and eventually to marry Catholics. The Chancellor's Club provided the opportunity for Catholic adults who were single to socialize and find a possible life partner. This club thrived until the downturn in all club activities in the late 1970s and the 1980s.

For Catholics studying at non-Catholic colleges and universities, the Newman Club program was expanded to virtually every major college in Washington. While Newman Clubs provided attractive liturgies, education in the faith, and an experience of community, they were unique venues for practicing the faith.

CYO,
Our Lady of Guadalupe Church,
Seattle

Chancellor's Club float, Seafair Parade

Catholic devotional life in the 1950s focused around Mary. The dogma of the Assumption of Mary into Heaven was defined in 1950, and 1954 was celebrated as a Marian year. In 1956 a diocesan-wide rosary crusade, included a rally at Husky Stadium attended by thousands, the highlight of which was the construction and recitation of the "living rosary."

In many parishes, devotions to Our Lady of Fatima were held on the first Saturday of each month; devotions to Our Lady of Guadalupe, were held in locations with concentrations of Hispanic/Latino Catholics. The months of October and May were months of special devotion to Mary. All Catholics were urged to say the rosary regularly. May processions were a familiar sight in Catholic parishes in the 1950s. The May crowning of the *Sedes Sapientiae* statue at St. Edward Seminary was a major event that lasted through the 1960s. The Legion of Mary continued to be as popular as it had been in the 1940s.

SEATTLE, WASHINGTON, FRIDAY, NOVEMBER 2, 1956 (Published every Friday)

Rosary Pledge Drive Opens Sunday

50,000 Attend Family Rosary Crusade Rally

LARGEST RELIGIOUS GATHERING in the history of Seattle took place Sunday when approximately 50,000 Catholics converged on the University of Washington Stadium to take part in the Family Rosary Crusade Rally conducted by Father Patrick Peyton, C.S.C., world-famous "Rosary Priest." A portion of the tremendous crowd is pictured above. Those taking part in the colorful procession which preceded the program are shown (top right) taking their places in the stands. In the foreground on the playing field, Catholic high school students form the "Living Rosary." Dominating the entire scene is the altar with a beautiful painting of the Blessed Virgin Mary on the tower in the background. Delegations from parishes in Seattle, Tacoma, Everett, Marysville, Bremerton, Bellevue, Port Angeles, Port Townsend and other near-by cities and towns attended the gigantic rally in a stirring demonstration of love and devotion to the Blessed Virgin. His Excellency, Archbishop Connolly presided at the rally and addressed the crowd briefly.

Rosary crusade rally at Husky Stadium, 1956

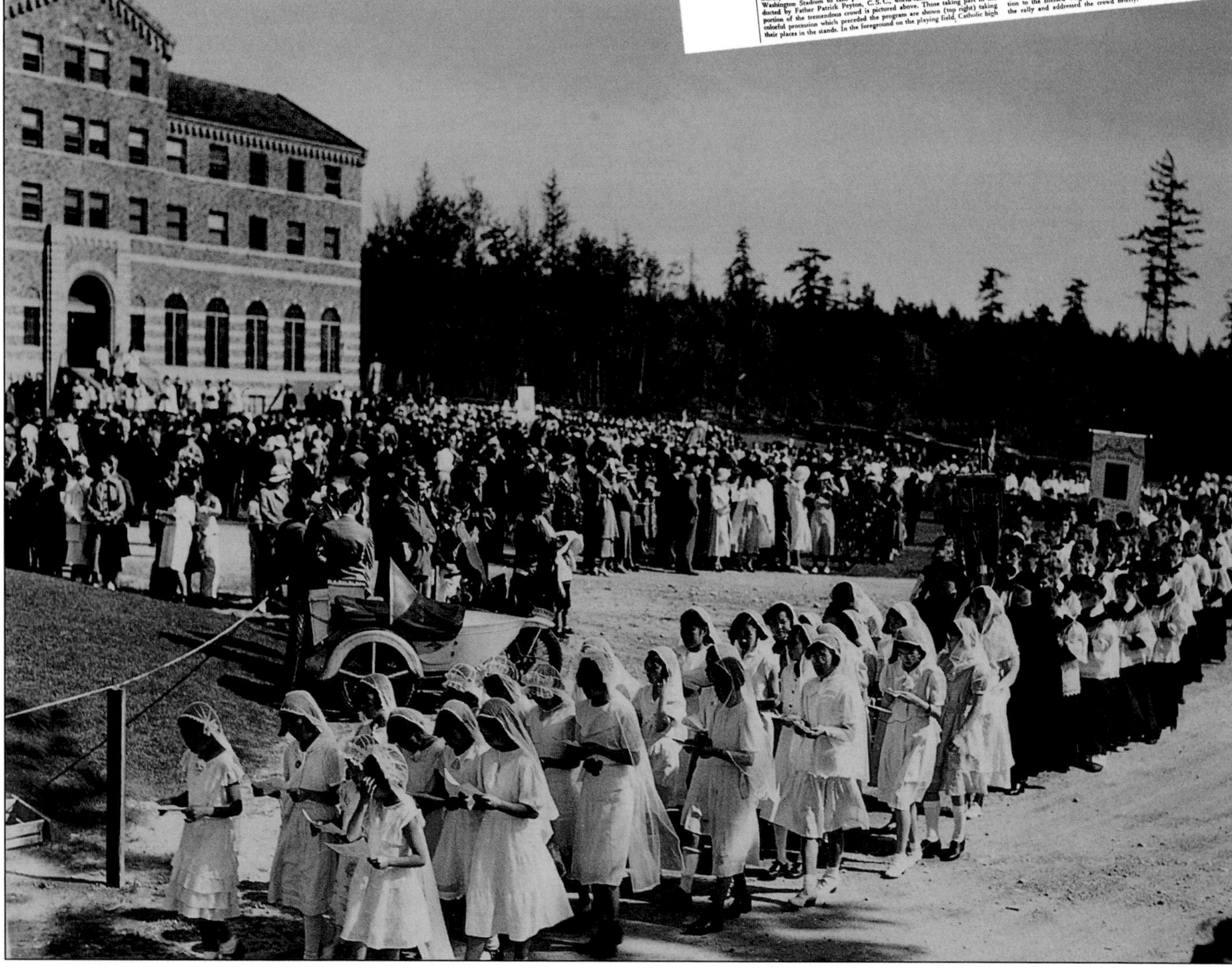

May Day procession, St. Edward Seminary, 1936

Religious communities promoted their distinctive devotions in parishes where they served: Jesuits promoted devotion to the Sacred Heart of Jesus; Franciscans to St. Francis and the Sorrowful Mother; Dominicans to Our Lady of the Rosary and St. Jude; and the Benedictines encouraged nocturnal adoration of the Blessed Sacrament. The Redemptorists sponsored Our Lady of Perpetual Help and the Carmelites Our Lady of the Scapular. If Mary and the saints remained daily companions, then the bridge between the devotional world and the increasingly modern and technologically shaped world of the 1950s could be maintained. The strain between the two was real, though often unacknowledged, in the lives of Catholic laity during the 1950s.

Devotional medal

New modes of devotion emerged that suggested things to come with the Second Vatican Council. The retreat movement grew after World War II. Most parishes sponsored or offered a weekend retreat for men and women at separate times of the years. Parish organizations also began to sponsor days of recollection. The popularity of the retreat movement indicated a strain that Catholic laity were experiencing in connecting their faith to their increasingly complex and professionally defined lives. It acknowledged that many Catholic laity needed and wanted formation in their faith that moved beyond devotional practice.

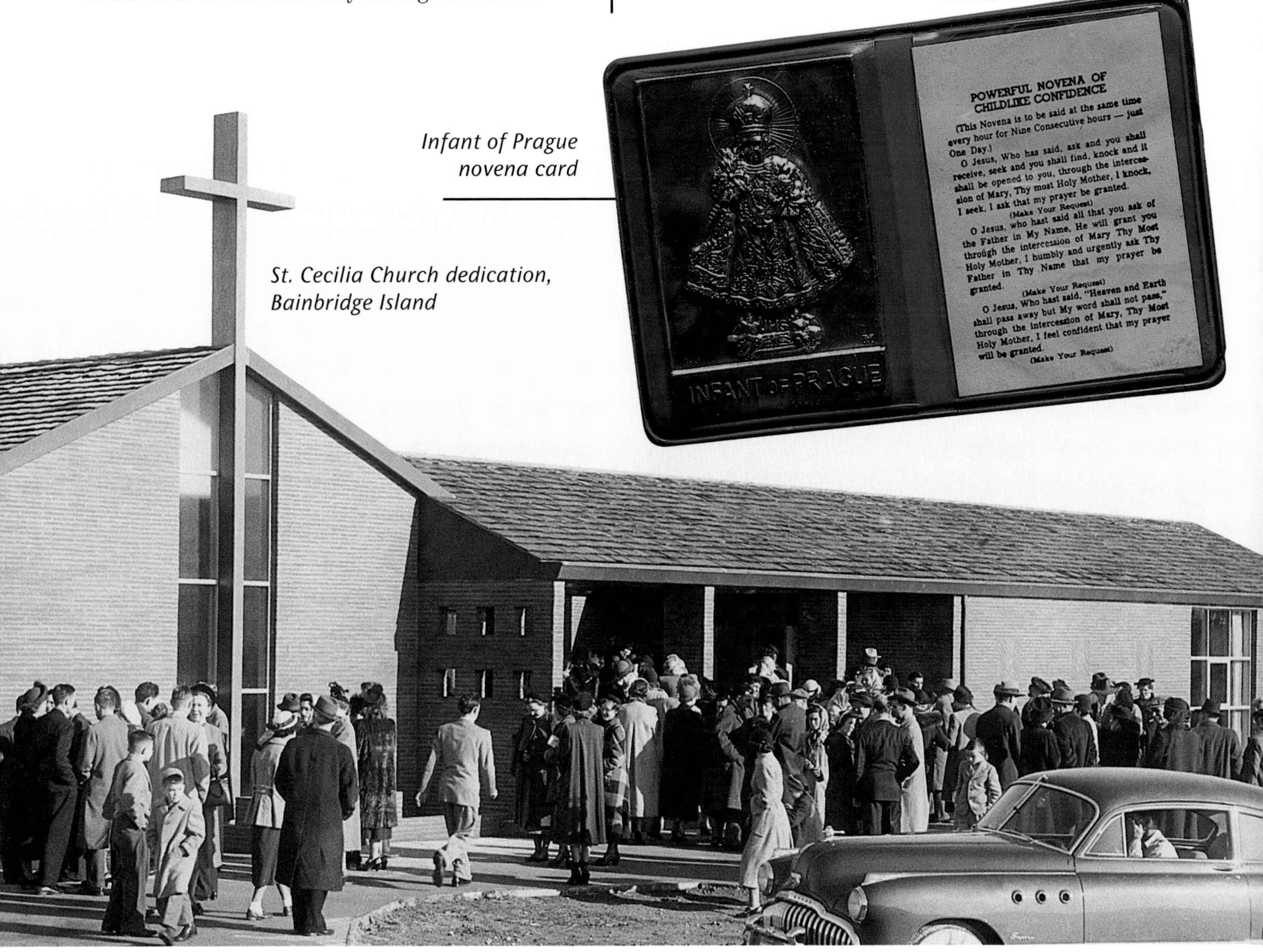

Infant of Prague novena card

St. Cecilia Church dedication, Bainbridge Island

Devotion to Our Lady of Fatima

The 1950s also saw changes in the liturgy. A few parishes experimented with the Dialogue Mass. By the late 1950s use of the English missal was as common during Mass as praying the rosary. In 1957 the fast prior to receiving holy Communion was reduced to three hours, allowing greater attendance at the Masses held later in the day and making frequent communion easier.

New organizations and educational programs appeared in parishes in the 1950s, though they would not spread widely until the 1960s. Marriage renewal and marriage education programs such as Cana and the pre-Cana Conferences became part of Catholic life. The Christian Family Movement, Young Christian Students, and Young Christian Workers all provided venues for Catholics to be engaged in specialized Catholic Action groups. In a few parishes, Living Room Dialogues were held, a movement that brought together people of various religious beliefs in small neighborhood groups to discuss doctrine. The purpose of these dialogues was understanding, not conversion. Some parishes held liturgy study groups. All these programs were designed to support laity to analyze and act in the world according to Catholic teaching. They required reflection and study on the part of their participants.

The newer devotions appealed to committed Catholic laity who were engaged in a major cultural shift. The war had brought Catholics out of their ethnic enclaves and into contact with people of multiple cultures and faiths.

Catholic War Veterans

The Catholic men who fought in the war and returned aspired to the "good life." A large number of these men went to college and made the shift from agricultural and blue-collar lives to professional and white-collar occupations. Seattle University illustrates the situation for Catholic colleges and universities across the country after World War II. In 1945 there were 900 full-time students at Seattle College (Seattle University). In 1946 there were 2,500 students, 1,300 of them war veterans, representing a 108% enrollment increase in one year. Beginning with this generation, the Catholic Church in the United States would become the most educated and affluent in the world. What this shift would mean for liturgical and devotional life, for magisterial teaching and authority, and for the persuasiveness of Catholic moral dictums would become clearer only in the mid-1960s.

Seattle University graduation, 1957

The Patrician Club at the Catholic Information Center with Fr. William Treacy (seated center)

Many Catholics in the 1950s were readers and an intellectual ferment not obvious to most Catholics until after Vatican II brewed. Catholics read novelists like Bruce Marshall and Graham Greene, Catholics who wrote about religious themes. Bishop Fulton Sheen was popular, presenting a Catholic intellectual synthesis that could guide life for Catholics and Protestants alike in the shadow of the nuclear threat. Catholic magazines were found in most Catholic homes. Catholic book clubs did good business. Parishes had lending libraries and discussion groups that met monthly to discuss the latest Catholic novel. Books and films about priests and nuns were popular, presenting in word and on screen what seemed to be ideal models of Catholic life.

Every respectable Catholic home had a crucifix, a statue of Mary, and in the best of them, a special kit so a priest could administer last rites. Catholics wanted to go to Catholic hospitals and most Catholics were buried in Catholic cemeteries.

Parish organizations continued to thrive in the 1950s, strengthened by the people's desire to return to normalcy, to catch up with dimensions

Lay Women's Group, 1954

Archdiocesan Council of Catholic Women, 1968

of their lives that had been interrupted by the war. The Holy Name Society, the Young Ladies' Institute, the Archdiocesan Council of Catholic Women, and the Knights of Columbus held Sunday morning breakfasts. Every Catholic woman knew that she automatically belonged to the Altar Society in her parish. Women's luncheons were immensely popular, also parish fashion shows. Even full-scale plays and musicals, more often than not directed by one of the parish priests marked the life of communities.

Knights of Columbus

Catholic laity in the 1950s knew that their faith offered guidance for life here and in the hereafter. While assertive evangelization was not the style for Catholics in the Northwest, the concern to share the faith with those searching for truth was very real. This led one convert, H.D. Norris, to become active in the Knights of Columbus and to suggest that Council 676 organize a Religious Information Bureau in Seattle. Seattle was the third diocese in the United States to have such a bureau. In the beginning, it reprinted a column "Catholic Information" provided by the Knights' Information Bureau of St. Louis. The purpose of the column was to stimulate thought and inquiry. Readers were invited to write to "Ralph C. Jackson" at a post office box in Seattle. In the early months there were only a few questions and Norris and his wife, Eva, composed the answers to inquiries, which then were checked by Father Joseph Dougherty, chancellor. But the number of inquiries grew and Norris appealed for help. The next to join were John McInerney and Louie Van Snyder. On Friday nights, the group gathered at the Norris home to compose responses.

Eventually, Father William Treacy was appointed chaplain for the group. Treacy suggested that the group write its own column for the newspapers, something more appropriate to the Northwest than those supplied by St. Louis. Thus, at its peak, the Seattle Knights of Columbus Religious Information Bureau received upward of 2000 inquiries a year. The group's men and women had various levels of education. All,

The Religious Information Bureau of the Knights of Columbus

however, were inspired by an experience of their faith that led them to share it with others, and in a way that would speak to everyday lives. These were people to whom Catholicism mattered and who knew it could make a difference.

The life of women religious changed in the 1950s as well. Women religious not only were the backbone of the Catholic education and health care systems in the United States, for large numbers of Catholics they symbolized what Catholicism meant. At the beginning of the 1950s, however, it was not clear how sisters, who had been an essential part of the immigrant church of the late 19th and early 20th centuries, fit in the post-war church. During the 1950s women religious began pursuing education, especially graduate education, in large numbers. They increasingly adopted professional standards for teaching, health care, and social work. Between 1950 and 1970, women religious became the most highly educated group of women in the United States.

During the 1950s new communities of women religious entered the archdiocese. In 1953, Sisters of Notre Dame de Namur returned after 109 years of absence. Archbishop Connolly also recruited Sisters of the Presentation of the Blessed Virgin Mary, who arrived in 1954 from San Francisco. In the same year members of the Congregation of the Sisters of the Holy Cross arrived in Seattle.

Sisters of St. Joseph of Peace, Seattle University

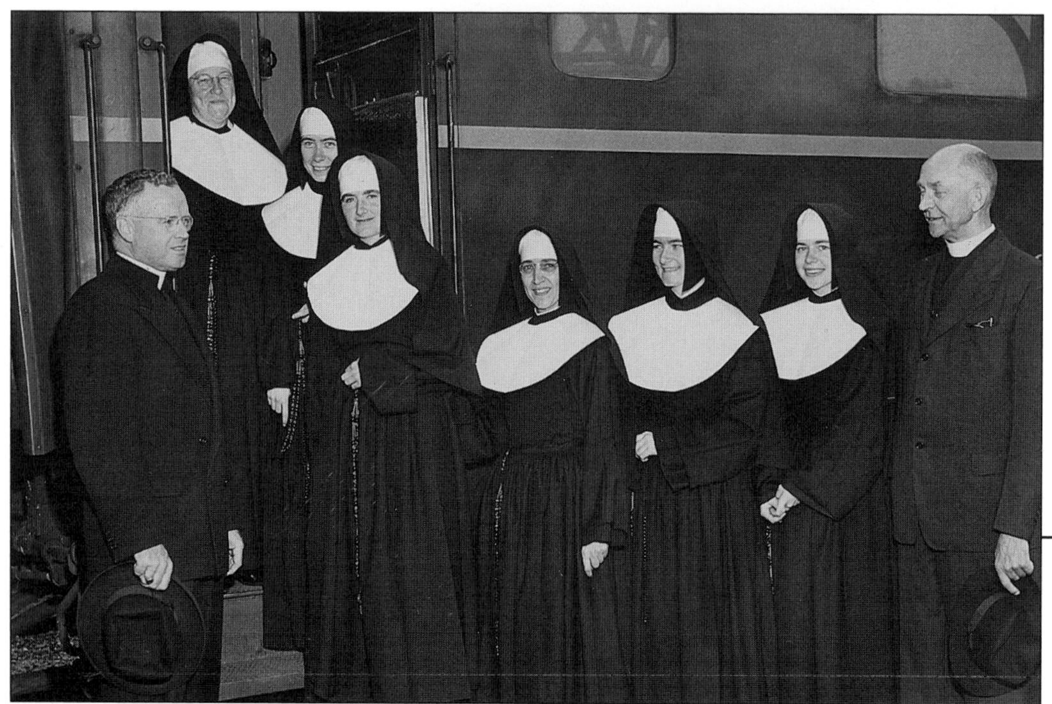

Return of the Sisters of Notre Dame de Namur

The growth and workload of the Archdiocese of Seattle were such that on April 11, 1956, Thomas Edward Gill, a native of St. Joseph Parish, Seattle, was appointed auxiliary bishop. Pastor of the Cathedral at the time of his appointment, Gill served as auxiliary until his unexpected death in 1973 at the age of 65. In many ways Bishop Gill's life mirrored the rapid changes of a century in the Archdiocese of Seattle. His parents were Irish immigrants who met in Seattle and married at our Lady of Good Help Church in 1890. Gill entered the minor seminary at the age of thirteen and completed priestly studies at St. Patrick's Seminary, Menlo Park, California. He was ordained on June 10, 1933, by Archbishop Hanna in St. Mary Cathedral, San Francisco. After graduate studies, he served the diocese in several administrative capacities, including director of Catholic Charities.

Many other young Catholic men of similar backgrounds entered the priesthood and experienced a similar shift in social and economic status. In the 1950s priesthood and religious life were attractive options. Connolly found himself in the enviable position of having sufficient vocations for the diocese. St. Edward Seminary had been designed for 111 students; in 1956 it had 256. This situation led Connolly to establish St. Thomas the Apostle Major Seminary. The cornerstone was

Thomas Gill preparing for installation as auxiliary bishop

St. Thomas the Apostle Seminary, Kenmore

laid on October 17, 1956. Construction began early in 1957 and in August 1958 the move of the major seminarians to the new facility was completed. The dedication of the new seminary took place on April 14, 1959.

A move toward professionalization in their apostolates became a concern of women religious in part as a response to concerns of Catholics and others about the quality of their schools, hospitals, and other institutions in the 1950s. Expectations for quality of service rose markedly in the 1950s. In summer, 1956, funded by a grant of $50,000 from the Fund for the Advancement of Education, fifteen participants, representing religious communities all over the United States, conducted the first national workshop on "Sister Formation," at the Providence School of Nursing in Everett. The president of Seattle University, Albert Lemieux, S.J., pledged support for the program. In the fall of 1957, a College of Sister Formation was set up at Seattle University as one of two national demonstration centers for the program, which the participants in the workshop had agreed upon. The five-year course of study was designed and the sisters attended four quarters each year. Women religious specialized in chosen fields.

The four communities in the Archdiocese of Seattle that participated in the movement were the Sisters of Providence, the Sisters of St. Joseph of Newark, the Dominican Sisters of the Congregation of St. Thomas Aquinas, and the Dominican Sisters of the Congregation of the Holy Cross. Other communities were influenced by the movement, though they did not join the venture. The dean of the new college was Mother Mary Philothea, S.P.

Providence Heights dedication, 1961 (l-r): Mother Mary Hildegarde, C.S.J., Rev. Albert Lemieux, S.J., Mother Judith, F.C.S.P., Archbishop Connolly, Most Rev. Egidio Vagnozzi (Apostolic Delegate), Mother Mary Philothea, F.C.S.P., Mother Mary Frances, O.P., Mother Mary Rosena, O.P.

On September 12, 1958, the *Catholic Northwest Progress* published a story of the plans for a new campus for the sister formation movement. Groundbreaking for Providence Heights College took place on January 21, 1959. The $6 million plant entailed nine separate buildings for 300 students and the provincial administration of the Sisters of Providence. The building was completed in 1961. That summer 256 sisters from thirty-six different communities began classes.

The sister formation movement attracted wide attention across the United States and abroad. The steps the sisters were taking to enhance their professional training both fascinated and disturbed many. It fascinated because it indicated change in the church and legitimated their own desires for better theological education and it disturbed because it indicated change. For the sisters, however, the movement prepared them for the directive to retrieve their founding charism and reflect on the meaning of vowed religious life in the modern world that would come to them out of Vatican II. It spurred the collaboration and cooperation among women religious across community lines that became a vital resource to these communities negotiating the changes and challenges of the post-Vatican II years.

While socialization of children and the desire to live a good Catholic life in a rapidly changing world marked the experience of Catholics in the 1950s, a theme that surrounded these concerns was the conflict with godless communism. The *Catholic Northwest Progress* put it this way in a June, 1950 editorial, "Conversion of Russia through prayer and reparation offered to God is the only sure way to bring lasting peace to the world." Lasting peace was desired by a generation that had learned what nuclear weapons could do. When Bishop Paul Yamaguchi of Nagasaki visited Seattle in January, 1955, Archbishop Connolly, on behalf of Catholics in the archdiocese gave him a check to aid those still suffering from the atomic blast of a decade earlier. The archbishop noted that "some 8,500 Catholics were among the 75,000 who died in the nuclear holocaust."

The desire to counter Communism pushed Church leaders to attend to Catholic social teaching and to support trade unions such as the Teamsters. During the 1950s, Connolly, through the *Progress*, repeatedly reminded Catholics of the Church's support for organized labor. Particularly when right-to-work initiatives were placed on the ballot, the archbishop would remind Catholics that the measures purposes weakened "…the power of organized labor to bargain collectively." In theory unions were acceptable to most Catholics, but in actuality to many Catholics they carried a taint of socialism and communism.

While in the early months of the 1950s Catholics spoke out against the arms race, the communist threat eventually brought most Catholic leaders into the mainstream in accepting, if not positively supporting, nuclear deterrence. As Father William Treacy described the 1950s, "We were so obsessed with communism, we forgot about everything else." Attention to the fight against communism at times prevented Connolly and the leadership of the archdiocese from attending to other significant challenges. However, the archdiocese joined with Plymouth Congregational Church in pushing the city to adopt an open-housing ordinance and promoted desegregation.

Throughout the 1950s, the African American/Black community in the archdiocese grew. Issues of adequate housing and discrimination in housing and employment became sharply pointed for the community in the 1950s. The majority of the African American/Black Catholics were members of St. Mary Parish or Immaculate Conception Parish in Seattle, the two parishes closest to the areas where they could secure housing. African American/Black Catholics, like their non-Catholic peers in Seattle in the 1950s, worked against the effort to deprive them of the gains in employment and social opportunity that World War II had occasioned.

Archbishop Connolly sought to provide social service ministry to his growing African American/Black community through the St. Peter Claver Center, which opened in what had been Our Lady Queen of Martyrs Parish. Bureaucratization and professionalization of archdiocesan social service ministries, begun under Shaughnessy's watch, continued throughout the 1950s.

St. Peter Claver Interracial Center

Korean orphans with Catholic Charities representatives, 1956

St. John Church, Vancouver, 1950

Mass at St. Catherine Church, Seattle

This reorganization of Catholic charitable work made it possible for the agencies to benefit from larger civic money-raising campaigns. In the 1930s Catholic Charities was a charter member of the United Good Neighbor Fund of King County. In the 1950s, Charities broadened its spectrum from focusing on orphans and disadvantaged youth, to work with the poor, the elderly, ethnic minorities, and refugees on issues of social services and housing. Archdiocesan Catholic Charities sponsored refugees from the 1956 Hungarian Revolution and would continue to sponsor refugees during the next forty years, from Korea, Vietnam, Cambodia, Laos, and other Pacific Rim nations.

A flurry of activity, abundant religious vocations, energetic Catholic laity, active participation in an array of devotional, social, and service groups, large Catholic families, a growing archdiocesan institutional structure to support ministries throughout the archdiocese—all were signs of a vital and triumphant Catholicism in the 1950s. All contributed to relief, to healing, to supporting the aspirations of Catholics coming to terms with the realities of World War II, the nuclear threat and to the continued existence of ethnic and racial prejudice in the nation.

But the world had changed. The wider experience, education, and altered social and economic context of Catholics after the war could not be undone. Underneath the surface of 1950s Catholicism, the realities of social injustice in American life and the increasing sophistication, education, and economic status of Catholic laity were, in small ways, intersecting with a Catholic biblical, historical, and theological renaissance. The Spirit was moving in the Church and would find voice in an elderly Italian cardinal, who would become known to the world as Pope John XXIII.

CHAPTER 6

TURMOIL AND THE LEADING OF THE SPIRIT, 1962-1975

St. Edward Church, Seattle

Vatican II opened in Rome, on October 11, 1962. Thomas A. Connolly had been a bishop for twenty-three years, and Archbishop of Seattle for twelve. Measured by bricks and mortar, personnel and programs, the archdiocese had achieved visible institutional success under Connolly's watch. More parish facilities were constructed during his tenure than had been built in the preceding 100-year history of the archdiocese. Vocations to the priesthood and to vowed religious life were abundant. Through Connolly and the programs of the archdiocese, the Roman Catholic Church in the Northwest was a presence in public discussion of labor rights, racial equality, open housing, and ecumenism. Catholic Charities continued to expand, providing ministries of care to families, orphans, unwed mothers, the aged, the infirm, refugees, and the poor. Lay organizations served as venues for Catholics to socialize with each other, reinforce Catholic identity, and provide service to the Church and the community.

Priests' retreat at St. Edward Seminary

St. Anne Church, Seattle

Our Lady of the Lake Church, Seattle

St. Patrick Church, Seattle

In a region where the church from the beginning had been challenged by geographic size, a small and dispersed population, and constant shortage of financial and personnel resources, Catholics in 1962 were proud of what they had built, proud to be Catholic, proud of their Catholic abundance. The Catholic Church in the Archdiocese of Seattle had arrived.

The Euro-Americans among Catholics of 1962 had experienced the Great Depression, proved their patriotism during World War II, and spent the 1950s establishing good lives for themselves and their families. They moved into the 1960s intending to enjoy life as American Catholics (for many in new homes in the suburbs) in relative tranquility, despite the backdrop of the Cold War. They were confident in their church and in how to be Catholic.

Many of the Archdiocese's African-American, Asian-American, and Hispanic/Latino Catholics entered the 1960s having shared in the Depression and World War II as well. But for them the experience had been different. Seattle's African American/Black Catholics, many of them relatively new to Washington State, having been attracted by employment possibilities or experiences at military bases in the region during World War II, entered the 1960s aware of continuing racism in the region and in the Church. Japanese-American Catholics entered the 1960s still suffering from their internment during World War II and the economic and social injustices that were part of that experience. Hispanic/Latino Catholics entered the 1960s as a growing population, but one largely invisible and economically and politically disenfranchised in society and in the Church.

On January 25, 1958, Pope John XXIII announced that he wanted "to offer to the Catholic Church and to the world the gift of a new Ecumenical Council." The Council's goal was *aggiornamento*, bringing the church up to date. Pope John wanted Catholicism to be sensitive to the larger historical and cultural contexts in which it preached the Good News. He wanted Catholic dogmas presented in the language of modern thought. Some among bishops, clergy, vowed religious and laity in the United States questioned the need for the Council. Archbishop Connolly was not among them. He departed for the opening session of the Council in October, 1962. He attended all four Council sessions. When he returned from the first session he pronounced himself a 'Vatican II bishop' and set about instituting the reforms for which the Council called.

Archbishop Connolly (center) attending a Vatican II session, 1963

■ THE SEATTLE BLACK CATHOLIC LAY CAUCUS

In 1970 a group of active African American/Black Catholic laity formed the Seattle Black Catholic Lay Caucus. Charter members who signed the articles of incorporation for the Caucus in 1971 were Solomon Gantt, Charmaine Hayes, James Henderson, and Walter T. Hubbard. Many of the Caucus' members also were active in the Knights and Ladies of Peter Claver. The Caucus' goals were to combat racism within and beyond the church and to promote the active involvement of African American/Black Catholic laity in the Archdiocese. Elizabeth Thomas captured the impetus for the organization as she reflected on her experience as a Catholic, "As it always is with Black Catholics, if you want to see change, you get involved."

The Caucus worked closely with Archbishop Thomas A. Connolly who endorsed its formation. Connolly saw the Caucus as a vehicle for "encouraging greater lay participation in church leadership activities by Black lay Catholics." He also considered the organization "a vehicle to identify and eradicate racism both within and outside of the church." The Caucus organized and promoted activities directed at achieving its goals and objectives. It established an office to facilitate its work and published a newsletter.

The Caucus focused attention on Catholic education in the archdiocese. It lobbied for increased numbers of students in Catholic schools and encouraged Connolly to provide scholarships for African American/Black students. It pushed for the recruitment and employment of African American/Black Catholics at the principal and administrative levels. The Caucus also provided consultation and support to parents who encountered difficulties within the Archdiocesan school system. Sometimes this involved providing an individual to assist with the investigation and resolution of the problem. During the 1970s, the Caucus worked against the closing of Immaculate Conception and St. Mary Schools in Seattle.

The Caucus sponsored its own educational programs through speakers, workshops, and training. It brought to Seattle the first five Black Bishops elevated in the United States, beginning with Bishop Harold Perry, who was ordained a bishop in 1965. The Caucus also sponsored workshops from its founding in 1970 until 1990. Events such as the 1972 "Teacher as a Catalyst for Change in Minority Education," and the 1985 "Multi-Cultural Participation in Church Life" were designed to identify and counteract racism in the Archdiocese.

The Caucus helped to support Fr. John Cornelius, the first African American/Black priest ordained for the Archdiocese of Seattle, during his years as a seminarian. When Fr. Cornelius arrived at Immaculate Conception Parish, he supported the work of the Caucus. The Seattle Black Catholic Lay Caucus lobbied for the creation of an African American/Black ministry position at the archdiocesan level. The first person to hold the position was Frances Woods. The Caucus also was active regionally and nationally. It lobbied for the creation of a National Office of Black Catholics and hosted a West Coast Conference of Black Catholics at Holy Names Academy in the early 1970s.

As Walter Hubbard commented on the organization in 1992, "We joined with the National Office of Black Catholics to share in a national effort to give a presence in what I call the Modern era of the Civil Rights Movement. This was a challenging time to giving birth to a national and local presence for Black Catholics who joined with their other brothers and sisters of Black America to overcome the vestiges of racism within the church and our country."

In the early 1990s a major concern and project for the Caucus was leadership training, formation, and development for young adults in the Archdiocese of Seattle. The Caucus wanted to instill in young adults a sense of commitment to the church, to family, and to social justice. In reflecting on the Caucus, Elizabeth Thomas noted that the Caucus had succeeded in getting an office of Black Catholics established, contributing to having more Black bishops ordained, and encouraging more Black seminarians. Over all the Caucus had succeeded in "identifying needs of Black Catholics" and "keeping them visible," to the point that "some clergy and bishops are responding." She is especially pleased on the regional level with the success of the gospel music choirs created by Black Catholics in the Archdiocese of Seattle. She sees these as a way to embody a truly "catholic" vision that is universal and so helps all in the church to embrace diversity.

Patricia Killen, Tacoma, WA

Neither Connolly nor his fellow Northwest bishops at the first session of the Council, among them Raymond G. Hunthausen of Helena, the youngest bishop at the Council, and Edward D. Howard of Portland, second oldest of the over 2,000 bishops and others who gathered in Rome, could have predicted its outcome. The Council's four sessions, focused on renewal in the Church and pastoral openness to the world, spanned four short years of rapid and radical disorientation in the United States. All the bishops who participated in Vatican II faced the challenging task of leading the Church through a process of renewal in an uncertain age. None escaped criticism for the work of the Council or for how they instituted its reforms in their dioceses.

Connolly wrote regularly from Rome to the people of the Archdiocese. Published in the *Catholic Northwest Progress*, the Archbishop's letters described to his flock the deliberations, liturgies, and decisions of the Council. He wrote in an engaging style that conveyed the excitement and hope of the Council even as he taught his people about development in a church that many of them had learned was an unchanging, timeless institution. Connolly's dispatches from the Council showed wit and pastoral sensitivity. In a way they began the process of preparing people for the changes to come.

The changes between 1962 and 1975 were many. In terms of the Council's actions, Catholics experienced change most in four major areas: liturgy, ministry and authority, ecumenism, and social justice. As these reforms were instituted they intersected with larger social movements to radically transform the face of the Church.

Historically the Catholic Church in the Archdiocese of Seattle has been flexible and receptive to change. Never has it had a sufficient concentration of population such that Catholics could avoid interacting with non-Catholics. From the beginning it had a tradition of strong lay leadership and lay initiative. Bishops and people knew that the Church's existence depended on laity's commitment and contributions. While sparse population,

Northwest (arch)bishops attending Vatican II: (l-r) Bernard Topel (Spokane), Thomas A. Connolly, Raymond Hunthausen (Helena), Sylvester Treinen (Boise)

large spaces, and few resources created challenges to establishing and maintaining institutions, these same factors contributed to an openness and flexibility on the part of Catholics in the archdiocese.

It was fitting, then, that the archdiocese hosted the 47th annual Liturgical Conference, convened on August 20, 1962, as the Catholic contribution to the Seattle World's Fair. The event was held in what is now the Key Arena. It was a very public Catholic event, a celebration of Catholic life in liturgy. Fifteen archbishops and bishops and 5,000 members of the clergy, religious orders, and laity gathered for lectures from nearly 100 distinguished speakers, discussion groups, and liturgies. In an act that presaged what was to come in the years after the Council, Connolly celebrated Mass facing the congregation at the closing liturgy of the Conference.

Vatican II brought Catholics a new understanding of the liturgy, one that accented meanings of the Eucharist that had been crucial in the early church but that had fallen into the background for many centuries. The language of the liturgy shifted from Latin to English. Laity's

Liturgical Conference, 1962

Sacred Heart Church tower and the Space Needle, Seattle

participation in the eucharistic celebration through prayer and song increased. The permanent diaconate was restored and married deacons became a fixture of parish life, both in liturgical celebrations and through ministry to the community.

Our Lady of Perpetual Help Church, Everett

Chalice

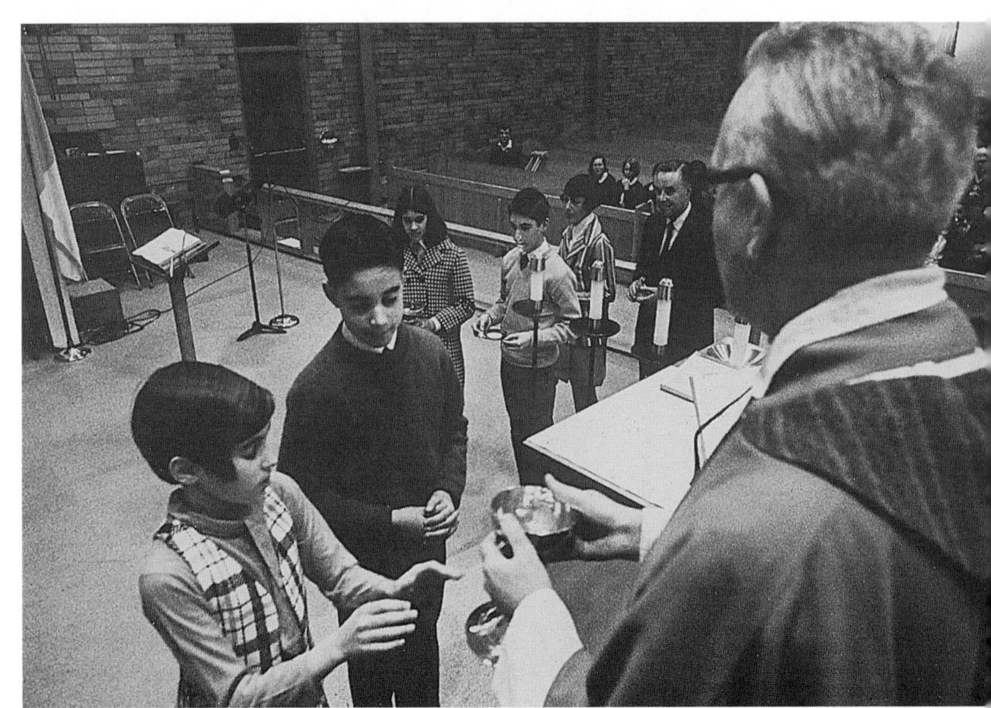

St. Luke Church, Shoreline

Vatican II led to revised presentation of all the sacraments. The Council reaffirmed the call to ministry of all God's people that is rooted in baptism. Confession became the rite of reconciliation of a penitent. Discussions ensued about the meaning of confirmation and the appropriate age for its reception. Extreme Unction became the anointing of the sick and was no longer reserved only for the moments before death. Matrimony was recast to highlight that this sacrament takes place between two people, witnessed, not performed, by the priest. The Rite of Christian Initiation of Adults was reintroduced into the Catholic Church. This process for preparing adults for baptism, with its accompanying rites, became a major renewal force in parish life across the United States. Father James Dunning of the Archdiocese of Seattle would go on to lead this initiative nationally through the North American Forum on the Catechumenate.

For some, the liturgical reforms were disorienting; for others, welcome. The turn toward Scripture and emphasis on spiritual development for adults enlivened their Catholicism and forged a connection between it and their daily lives. Study groups, especially Scripture study groups, increased in number across the archdiocese. Prayer services developed from Scripture and focused around contemporary social issues appeared in parishes alongside the more traditional practices of novenas and rosaries.

The structure of parishes changed. Pastoral councils, finance councils, liturgical committees, education committees, social justice committees and more were established in parishes. Collaboration between laity and clergy became the goal for parish life. Catholic schools shifted from the responsibility of the religious communities that staffed them to programs within the parish.

Parish council, St. Mary Church, Seattle

The configuration of parish staffs changed as well. Communities of women religious, responding to the Council's call to reclaim their original charisms, expanded their range of ministries. Many left elementary and secondary classrooms to work with the poor and marginalized. Lay teachers stepped in to fill the gap. Some parish schools were forced to close in the early 1970s, a consequence of multiple factors, including the loss of women religious, increasing costs, inflation, and a regional recession. The situation stabilized by the mid 1970s as pastors, lay school boards, and dedicated parents ensured the continued success of Catholic education.

Martin Luther King Jr. Daycare Center, Seattle

The decade following Vatican II saw the beginning of a proliferation of full-time ministry positions in parishes that were filled by laity. The first positions to appear were religious education coordinators and directors of religious education. The need for these positions came, in part, from the realization that population increases were outstripping the ability of parishes to provide schools for all Catholic children. In 1965 such positions did not exist in the archdiocese.

A special edition of the *Catholic Northwest Progress* explained the role to readers in 1969. The responsibilities of coordinators or directors included CCD pre-school, elementary and secondary, parent education, home visitation, neighboring parish programs, continuing adult formation, adult discussion clubs, teacher training, parent-teacher programs, parochial schools, and ministry of good will, all done with the support of the archdiocesan religious education office. The level of professional

'Go teach all nations'

Joseph C. Harris, (above), Religious Education Coordinator at Holy Trinity Parish, Bremerton, typifies the way Christ's command to "Go forth and teach all nations" is being followed in our day. The command remains unchanged, but times and places have changed, making it necessary to adopt new techniques and forms for the spreading of the Gospel.

Vol 72, Easter Edition — April 1, 1969 — No. 14

Northwest Progress

Religious education supplement, the Catholic Northwest Progress, *1969*

Our Lady of the Lake School, Seattle

training varied among religious education coordinators throughout the archdiocese. Archbishop Connolly included a statement expressing "unqualified approval and endorsement" of the role of religious education coordinators.

Seattle University, in cooperation with the archdiocese, responded to the need for theological education for lay professionals in the church by instituting and expanding programs in theology. In 1969 it introduced FIRE, a graduate program which incorporated "an interdisciplinary blending of . . . theological knowledge, with insights from the social sciences and communications skills." Persons successfully completing the program received masters degrees in religious education,

By 1975 religious education had spawned specializations that became independent ministries in many parishes—youth ministry, family ministry, and formation ministry. The evolution of these independent ministries out of religious education reflected a growing sophistication among pastors and teachers in their understanding of how religious identity is shaped and sustained.

Youth ministry programs, related to but different from the earlier and continuing CYO program of the archdiocese, provided opportunities for spiritual development such as the Search Program designed to provide peer ministry, encouragement, and identity in the faith. Similarly, family ministry programs, rooted theologically in the family as the domestic church, also responded to the shifting realities of families in the United States. The emergence of new ministries, staffed by lay men and women, both married and vowed religious, changed the landscape of parish life and the way that Catholics thought about their spiritual development and their faith.

Mass, CYO Camp

1962 to 1975 saw the growth, decline, and adjustment of many lay organizations in the archdiocese. These events had more to do with larger social factors than with the organizations themselves. The increasing entry of women into the work force decreased the number of women available for participation in clubs and other voluntary organizations that had been part of parish life for many decades.

Mass at Our Lady of Guadalupe Church, Seattle

While traditional organizations continued, new organizations came onto the scene, including those for professionals such as religious educators or youth ministers, special interest organizations, organizations that focused on spiritual development, and organizations focused on the Church's social justice teachings. Some of these groups were led by priests and religious who, in response to Vatican II, felt called to share their particular spiritual traditions with laity. Others were spiritual development groups that

Sanctuary Club, St. John Church, Seattle

Knights of Columbus with Fr. James Eblen, 1967

Challenge program panelists (l-r): Dr. Lynn Corson, Rabbi Raphael Levine, Fr. William Treacy

grew out of lay movements, such as Cursillo, a contribution from the Hispanic/Latino community, and Marriage Encounter. Thus, new organizations and new ministries became part of Catholic life in the 1960s and 1970s.

Another development of Vatican II that had an even wider impact beyond the confines of parish life was Catholic openness to ecumenism. The Archdiocese of Seattle had a history of ecumenical activity, born of the frontier setting.

Connolly had endorsed ecumenism during his episcopacy and had participated in the Church Council of Greater Seattle. With the announcement of Vatican II, however, Connolly reconsidered a 1952 invitation from Rabbi Raphael Levine to participate in a television program that would bring together a Roman Catholic priest, Rabbi Levine, and a Protestant minister to discuss theological and social issues. Levine proposed the program as a way to combat religious intolerance and promote interfaith understanding. The archbishop appointed Father William Treacy to join the Rabbi on KOMO's *Challenge* program. The Protestant participant, originally Dr. Martin Goslin of Plymouth Congregational Church, rotated and so Treacy and Levine became the dominant personalities on the program. The second Protestant panelist was Dr. Lynn Corson of University Methodist Temple. He was followed by Pastor Oscar Rolander, a Lutheran, and then Dr. Robert Fine, Pastor of the Free Methodist Church at Seattle Pacific University.

The *Challenge* program lasted for fourteen years and had an audience of 300,000 persons each week. The representatives of the three faiths that shared difficult and painful histories discussed issues that divided them in a lively, rational, and amiable manner. The program did not shy away from difficult issues. Among the topics discussed were having a Catholic president; who bore responsibility for crucifying Jesus; open housing in Seattle; moral challenges to youth; and celebrating Christmas in public schools. KOMO's *Challenge* program became a national model for interfaith conversation.

The friendship between Levine and Treacy was recognized nationally when the media covered the installation of the altar in Treacy's new parish, St. Patrick, Seattle, an altar carved at Treacy's request by Levine. Treacy and Levine shared more than a long friendship of mutual respect. The two men also shared a vision of interfaith cooperation and dialogue and an assumption that the spiritual experience of people is the starting point for overcoming prejudices and animosity. Their dream became embodied in Camp Brotherhood, located near Mt. Vernon, Washington, aimed at promoting interfaith cooperation between families. Though Rabbi Levine died in November, 1985, Treacy carries on their work for interfaith unity at Camp Brotherhood.

Archbishop Connolly with Arthur Ramsey, Archbishop of Canterbury, Sept. 24, 1967

Treacy served as chairman of the Commission for Church Unity from 1965 through 1975. Those years were momentous for opening up conversation between the archdiocese and other Christian bodies in the region. Local parishes held conversations with Protestant churches near them. In some cases pastors and congregations also engaged in dialogue with Jewish representatives of local synagogues. Ecumenical discussions extended and developed cooperation among denominations on social issues. In April, 1972, the archdiocese joined with twelve other denominations in an "Ecumenical Witness for Peace" gathering held in Seattle. The organization focused on the Vietnam War.

Ministries of justice, primarily addressing poverty and racial discrimination, began to emerge within the archdiocese. Members of religious communities engaged in these ministries as part of their process of retrieving and

Catholic Interracial Council banquet

grounding themselves once again in the charism of their founders. The archdiocese also developed peace and justice ministries during this time.

Fighting for the civil rights of African American/Blacks was one area where representatives of the church, including priests such as Rev. D. Harvey McIntyre, the first Executive Director of the Washington State Catholic Conference, worked for justice. The Catholic Interracial Council promoted the desegregation of Seattle's schools, open housing, and civil rights for African American/Blacks. Its activities were covered fully in the *Progress*. Connolly spoke out against red-lining, the practice of refusing loans to African American/Blacks in order to keep them from moving into specific neighborhoods. He had endorsed a boycott of public schools because of discrimination against African American/Blacks. He required that all construction projects for the archdiocese include a clause forbidding discrimination in hiring workers. Connolly also initiated Project Equality, which committed archdiocesan institutions to buy goods from firms that pledged Affirmative Action.

On issues involving civil rights, open housing, and equal employment, Connolly often cooperated

Catholic Interracial Council 1968 banquet with Archbishop Connolly (c), Bishop Harold Perry of New Orleans (r), and Bishop Ivol Curtis of the Episcopal Diocese of Olympia (l)

Interfaith prayer service held in honor of the recently assassinated Dr. Martin Luther King Jr., April 12, 1968

with prominent Baptist leader, Rev. William McKinney. Throughout the 1960s civil rights marches in Seattle were ecumenical and interracial affairs. African American/Black Catholics and some clergy and religious participated actively in these marches which were organized and led by pastors of parishes such as Immaculate Conception and St. Mary in Seattle.

In 1974, Joseph McGowan, S.J., became the first African American/Black priest ordained in the archdiocese. In 1975, John Cornelius was ordained. Seattle's African American/Black community took a blow in the 1970s when the parochial schools at St. Mary and Immaculate parishes were closed. These schools had been major centers for the community, vehicles of Catholic evangelization in the African American/Black community, and ministries of social justice for the church. At the same time, the Knights of Peter Claver and Ladies Auxiliary

Ordination of Joseph McGowan, S.J., first African American/Black priest ordained in the archdiocese, 1974

enjoyed a growth in popularity among the African American/Black Catholic community. Seattle's tradition of strong lay leadership carried over into the national sphere when Clayton Pitre and Cheryl Adams provided national leadership to the Black Catholic Lay Caucus.

The years 1962-1975 were significant for the growing Hispanic/Latino Catholic community in the archdiocese as well. Nearly 40,000 people with Spanish surnames moved to Puget Sound between 1940 and 1980, most coming after 1960. More than 80% were of Mexican ancestry. Most were born in the southwestern United States and moved from Texas and California, to Colorado, into eastern Washington and then the Yakima Valley. Just as for the African American/Black community, employment opportunities created by World War II brought Hispanic/Latinos to Washington. In the 1950s, a few left the Yakima Valley for Seattle and better opportunities. The migration across the Cascades increased during the 1960s and 1970s.

Those who had come before, such as Roberto Gallegos, helped the newcomers. Gallegos spearheaded the creation of a community center for Hispanic/Latinos, El Centro de la Raza, that would provide needed services for the stream of new residents. Chicanos and other Latinos pressed for affirmative action at educational institutions such as the University of Washington. A growing network of Mexican businesses began to dot the landscape of Puget Sound.

Culturally the majority of Hispanic/Latinos who came to Puget Sound were Roman Catholic. Providing liturgy and pastoral care in Spanish became a priority of the archdiocese in the 1970s. Hispanic/Latino Catholics and others concerned for justice were involved during these years with the plight of farm workers and the efforts of César Chávez and the United Farm Workers to gain improvements in wages and working conditions. In the late 1970s and the 1980s Hispanic/Latino Catholics and their allies in the archdiocese were involved in the Sanctuary Movement, assisting refugees from Central America.

With continuing waves of immigration from a range of Latin countries, each with distinct cultures, over long periods of time, the Hispanic/Latino communities face intergenerational strains that assimilation presents to all immigrants. At the parish and archdiocesan level the Church has sought to assist these new immigrants.

Beginning in the 1960s the archdiocese experienced new waves of Asian and Pacific Island immigration as well. Hawaiians who worked for the Hudson's Bay Company were present in the region when the first missionaries arrived in 1838. Filipinos as well were in the region, often as workers on ships. The Chinese came in large numbers during the 1870s and 1880s, primarily working on the railroads. The Japanese immigration had peaked from the turn of the 20th century until the restriction on immigration laws in the 1920s. Post-1960 Vietnamese, Laotian, Cambodian, Samoan, and other Asian and Pacific Americans arrived in the archdiocese. Catholic Charities participated actively in refugee resettlement. Archdiocesan programs offered liturgical and pastoral care for the new immigrants and incorporated their distinctive devotions and liturgical practices into parish life. Sensitivity to new Asian and Pacific American arrivals led to deeper appreciation of the distinctive cultural practices of those who had been here longer, such as the Filipinos, Koreans, and Japanese.

Asian and Pacific American Heritage Month celebration, JFK High School, Burien, 1997

Refugee settlement program, Our Lady of Mount Virgin Church, Seattle

In 1975, Connolly retired. He had led the archdiocese when it was strong and confident in its identity. He had led the archdiocese through the implementation of the reforms called for by Vatican II. He sought to practice responsible episcopal leadership and authority during decades when most Americans, including Catholics, were questioning institutional authority and the value of tradition. He oversaw the transformation of parish and diocesan staff from primarily clergy and religious to lay people. He grieved the number of priests and women religious who left religious life as well as the beginning of a series of closings of institutions that had embodied Catholicism for so many—schools, hospitals, orphanages. Archbishop Connolly retired, knowing that the turmoil and challenge would continue for his successor.

On February 25, 1975, Raymond G. Hunthausen of the Diocese of Helena was transferred to the Archdiocese of Seattle. He was installed on May 22, 1975, as the sixth bishop and second archbishop of Seattle in a ceremony at Seattle's Civic Center. Having been mentored by Bishop Bernard Topel of Spokane, Hunthausen's style was different from Connolly's. His deep commitment to a life of simplicity led him to live at the Cathedral rectory rather than at the archbishop's residence. Hunthausen's commitment to peace and against weapons of war would lead to a confrontation with people in the archdiocese. It would inspire many others, both in the Catholic Church and beyond.

Hunthausen's installation, May 22, 1975

Raymond G. Hunthausen

CHAPTER 7

CARRYING THE GIFT OF FAITH INTO THE TWENTY-FIRST CENTURY, 1975-2000

The last twenty-five years have been a time of increased understandings and perspectives about what it means to be the people of God, going about the work of the reign of God in our region and our world.

In reflecting on her years in religious life, Tacoma native Sr. Lucy Wynkoop, O.S.B., of St. Placid's Priory, explained how in the

wake of Vatican II's call for renewal the first steps were taken on the visible level, perhaps most pointedly for women religious in the process of modifying the habit. "Discussing the habit covered what we did not know how to say."

During the 1970s, Benedictines began reclaiming their charism and continued in the 1980s studying the meaning of monasticism. The focus at St. Placid's had shifted from the ministry of education in parochial schools to community and prayer, with ministries of education, spiritual direction, and other forms of service emerging out of that deep and defining well of Benedictine life. At the year 2000 the community of women at St. Placid's, Lacey, focuses around a common understanding of the fundamental impulse and call of monastic life and seeks to be faithful to the question, "What is our charism and how do we make it applicable for the needs of the world today?" As they live and respond to that question, other women join them, attracted by a life of deep faithfulness and the ministries that arise from it.

Since 1975, the Church has experienced a growing spiritual revival, a product of the search for meaning against the challenging backdrop of reform. Catholics have sought to maintain a vital faith in very different circumstances from those of their parents or grandparents.

The growing understanding of the Catholic faith as it is received, experienced, and lived in particular human communities, especially distinctive ethnic communities, has proven to be as important as the renewal of spirituality and the concern for justice. In the late 1960s, the 1970s and 1980s, ethnic communities, inspired by the call for justice and the norm of respect and dignity for all peoples, voiced their concerns about injustice toward minority peoples in the

St. Placid Priory, Sisters of St. Benedict, July 1992

church. African American/Black Catholics, Hispanic/Latino Catholics, and Asian and Pacific American Catholics have created and demanded representation and participation in leadership and pastoral roles in the national and local Church.

Out of these family struggles, the Church in the U.S. has aspired to embody the commitment to appropriately shared authority. Laity are now routinely invited to participate in local decision-making where their experience is the agent of Christian community. Pastoral councils, finance councils, and other parish and diocesan-based consultative bodies have grown as a result.

In 1975 the Catholic population of the Archdiocese of Seattle was nearly 350,000 (approximately 10%) out of a total state population of 3,421,593. In 1999 the Catholic

St. Therese Church, Seattle

Mary Jane Kobayashi and Tom Kobayashi

Samoan Catholics at Asian and Pacific American Annual Gathering, 1997

population of the archdiocese was estimated at 516,000 (approximately 12%) out of a total state population of 4,485,800. But while the Catholic population has grown rapidly during these twenty-five years, the total number of parishes, missions, and faith communities has not. The number of parishes, missions, and faith communities has increased from 166 in 1970 to 174 in 1999. The region's growth and renewal have created opportunities to move in new directions and a necessary commitment to broader collaboration among clergy, religious, and laity, in responding to the pastoral and spiritual needs of Catholics in the archdiocese.

Fr. Michael Holland, St. Charles Church, Burlington

Vietnamese Lunar New Year celebration, St. James Cathedral

Korean celebration of the Mass, St. Ann Church, Tacoma

The archdiocese has been led by three archbishops during 1975-2000. Raymond G. Hunthausen was appointed archbishop on February 25, 1975, and retired on his 70th birthday, August 21, 1991. Thomas J. Murphy was appointed coadjutor archbishop on May 26, 1987, succeeded Hunthausen on August 21, 1991, and died June 26, 1997. Alexander J. Brunett is the fourth archbishop and eighth bishop of Seattle. He was appointed on October 28, 1997 and installed at St. James Cathedral on December 18, 1997.

Concern for justice, inclusiveness, the poor, and respect for and celebration of multi-culturalism inside and outside the Church has been evident in diocesan and parish-based programs, and through the leadership of Archbishops Hunthausen and Murphy, and now through Archbishop Alex J. Brunett. They have been assisted by auxiliary bishops who have shared the responsibilities for the archdiocese. Nicholas Walsh assisted Hunthausen from 1976 until Walsh's resignation in 1983. Donald W. Wuerl was appointed auxiliary bishop on November 30, 1985, ordained by Pope John Paul II on January 6, 1986, and appointed and canonically installed as Bishop of Pittsburgh on February 12, 1988. George L. Thomas is the newest auxiliary bishop in the archdiocese, as well as the vicar general. Bishop Thomas was appointed November 19, 1999 and ordained on January 28, 2000 at St. James Cathedral.

Archbishops Raymond G. Hunthausen (r) and Thomas J. Murphy

Bishop George Thomas at Holy Rosary Church, Edmonds

Aware of the need for the local Church to express its embodiment of the Catholic faith, Archbishops Hunthausen and Murphy each published vision statements formulated in consultation with an Archdiocesan Pastoral Council. These statements sought to articulate the identity and mission of the Roman Catholic Church in Western Washington. Hunthausen's *"To Reflect His Light: The Goals of the Roman Catholic Church in Western Washington, 1981-1985"* and *"The Love of Christ Compels Us: The Priorities and Goals of the Roman Catholic Church of Western Washington, 1986-1990,"* and Murphy's *"A New Wind and Fire: A Vision Statement for the Years 1995-2000 A.D., Archdiocese of Seattle"* have provided educational and institutional efforts to expand awareness of gifts for ministry and opportunities for offering those gifts to others. Archbishop Brunett is currently in the process of convening an Archdiocesan Pastoral Council for the first years of the 21st century.

Archbishop Hunthausen greeting parishioners

Archbishop Hunthausen encouraged the formation of pastoral councils and the cultivation of lay leadership in parishes and faith communities throughout the archdiocese. Ministerial development programs of various forms were created and implemented to help people experience more acutely their particular ministries as members of the church. Faith and community development programs, CYO, religious education, and specialized ministries to ethnic minorities and the disabled were enhanced or developed. The Archdiocese became known for pioneering efforts in helping young adults identify and pursue vocations in the church, as laity as well as clergy and vowed religious. The CHANNEL Program became a model for such efforts in other dioceses. Lay organizations grew in number and diverse character as well. Traditional groups continued to exist, yet others emerged. Groups such as the Association of Religious Educators of the Archdiocese of Seattle, Seattle Black Catholic Lay Caucus, Cursillo Movement, Association for Lay Ministers, and Western Washington Catholic Charismatic Renewal illustrated a shift toward interest in spirituality, the political sphere, and the professionalization of ministry.

Carolyn Drobnicki, who has Downs Syndrome, during the "Inclusion Weekend" at Holy Family Parish in Kirkland, in 1995. Fr. Robert Camuso and Fran Drobnicki, Carolyn's mother, are in the background.

A renewed focus on vocations to ordained and vowed religious life has generated a call to identify and support these gifts for ministry. The World Day of Prayer for Vocations on April 27, 1980 was marked in the archdiocese by special activities and a supplement in the *Catholic Northwest Progress. "Good Ground, Good Seed"* described the array of ministry training programs for future clergy, religious, and lay ministers. Archbishop Murphy, and now Archbishop Brunett, have encouraged the Catholic people of the archdiocese to consider service to the Church, especially vocations to ordained ministry. Archbishop Murphy was Chair of the Committee on Priestly Formation as well as Chair of the Committee on Priestly Life and Ministry for the National Conference of Catholic Bishops. His interest and dedication to priestly vocations began a gradual upswing in the number of seminarians for the archdiocese. In 1990 the number of seminarians was thirteen; today there are thirty. The last permanent deacon ordinations took place in 1989. In 1990, Archbishop Hunthausen suspended the program, which was under review when Archbishop Murphy became ill. In response to changing pastoral needs, Archbishop Brunett re-established the archdiocesan Deacon Formation Program following comprehensive consultation with clergy, religious, and laity. In January, 2000, thirty-one applicants were accepted into the program.

Renewal and change also have marked religious communities during the past twenty-five years. As communities aged and fewer persons entered, religious have worked to make sure their original vision continues in their organizations, such as hospitals and schools. At the same time they have worked to develop ways to invite laity into their ministries on short- and long-term bases. Cooperation among religious communities has also proven effective. The Intercommunity Center for Peace and Justice is an example of efforts to promote education and action on these issues. Women religious and lay persons have become involved more extensively in parish professional ministry as educators, pastoral ministers, and administrators. Sisters Elizabeth Joyce, S.P. and Virginia Miller, S.P., pioneered parochial ministry in the predominantly rural settings of Pe Ell and Aberdeen. Permanent deacons also have become more visible in parishes in the past twenty-five years as well, in the areas of liturgy, outreach, and administration.

Daniel Allen, deacon, St. John Bosco Church, Tacoma

Ordination of James Johnson (l) and Derek Lappe (r), with Archbishop Brunett and Bishop Thomas, June 10, 2000

The 1970s was a time of considerable transition in Catholic parochial education. Because of the rapid shift in school staff from religious to laity coupled with the economic challenges of the times, some schools were closed. The creativity and commitment of laity and clergy in parishes, along with archdiocesan concern and support, allowed grade schools and high schools to adapt to the new situation, so that Catholic education is dynamic and growing today. In 1979, Archbishop Hunthausen published a pastoral letter on Catholic education. He acknowledged that the late 1960s and early 1970s were a difficult time for Catholic schools because of soaring costs and declining enrollments. The archbishop was able to point out in his letter, however, that once a first-grader entered a Catholic school that child's chance of graduating from a Catholic school was more than 90%. By 1990 new schools such as Archbishop Thomas J. Murphy High School in Everett and Eastside Catholic High School in Bellevue had opened.

Under Archbishop Murphy's leadership a major study of Catholic schools in the archdiocese was undertaken. The recommendations of the study included goals to guide Catholic schools into the 21st century.

Immaculate Conception/ Our Lady of Perpetual Help School, Everett

St. Paul School, Seattle

Holy Rosary Church, Seattle

The same energy and commitment to forming young Catholics was devoted to youth ministry and catechesis for those Catholic children in public schools as well. In the 1970s and 1980s the archdiocese and parishes worked to improve the quality of catechesis for Catholic children, to provide youth ministry opportunities even beyond the traditional CYO programs, and to help children, young adults, and families to reflect on and strengthen their Catholic faith. Energies and resources directed toward a commitment to the catechesis and formation of Catholic youth continued in the 1990s.

On issues of peace and justice, Archbishop Hunthausen became known for his strong stance opposing nuclear weapons. In 1982 he announced that he would withhold half his income tax in protest; the IRS garnished his wages as a result. In 1983, Archbishop Hunthausen was the focus of an apostolic visitation looking into a number of administrative and pastoral practices. The process would last six years, two years of which Auxiliary Bishop Donald Wuerl was assigned to assist the archbishop in certain areas. The visitation process resulted in the appointment of a coadjutor archbishop in 1987.

Hunthausen wearing stole from Lao tribal communities

December 16, 1982 The Progress 3A

The hopes of the human family center around peace

My Dear Sisters and Brothers:

Once again the ordinary routine of daily living makes way for Christmas. All over the world people take comfort in the underlying message of Christmas. It is a message of hope – hope that life, after all, is immensely precious, and hope that however fearful the future may appear, the deepest dreams and longings of the human heart will one day be fulfilled.

Perhaps as never before, today the hopes of the human family center around peace – that profound and all-embracing peace which is of God, and for which the Prince of Peace was born.

The absence of peace is all too evident. The millions in our nation who look in vain for employment, experiencing in each rejection the increased sense of personal futility, know the absence of peace. People who are cold and hungry this Christmas season, and who see no relief in sight, know the absence of peace. Senior citizens living alone at a level of bare subsistence, young people lacking funds for a college education, ethnic minorities struggling for acceptance in society, the sick and the imprisoned, know the absence of peace.

Beyond such circumstances, which touch only the less fortunate among us, there looms a worldwide problem affecting everyone: a growing resort to violence in order to pursue peace. The violence in northern Ireland is carried on by both parties as a means for gaining peace. The Beirut massacre, a modern-day slaughter of the innocents, was a perverse effort to ensure peace. The escalating violence in Latin America, the carnage in Afghanistan, and the daily upheavals in Africa, are flamed by a thirst for peace.

More ominous still, among the powerful nations of the world nuclear stockpiles continue to be enlarged in irrational proportions. Too, each year an increasing number of poorer nations divert their precious resources into developing a nuclear capability in the vain hope that the avenue to peace is the threat of war. Inevitably, the entire human family faces a heightening specter of eventual massive destruction.

Given the darkness enveloping this Christmas of 1982, one may feel that its message of hope no longer applies. The opposite is true. Etched by shadows, the summons of the Lord of Light to renewed hope stands out all the more starkly.

There is cause for despair only if we Christians lose faith in the birth of Christ, or in his power to save. In

Archbishop Raymond G. Hunthausen

the Christmases preceding this one, the failure of peace for the world has been a failure of faith – a failure to take at face value God's revelation to us through Jesus. Perhaps we are now prepared to truly listen to what our heavenly Father tells us through his Son. Perhaps this Christmas, at last, will mark the dawning of that peace proclaimed for humankind on the first Christmas night.

What does God tell us through his Son? He tells us that the only path to lasting peace is the eradication of violence in all of its destructive forms. It is a difficult message. But it is a clear one: "You have learned how it was said: You must love your neighbor and hate your enemy. But I say this to you: love your enemies and pray for those who persecute you" (Mt. 5:43-44). Jesus fulfilled these words to the letter; he yielded without protest to his executioners, and prayed: "Father, forgive them; they do not know what they are doing" (Lk. 23:24). Because Jesus was faithful to the cause of God's peace to the very end, he was raised up to become the source of everlasting peace for the entire human family.

To be a Christian is to be a disciple of Jesus – one who consciously tries to follow Jesus throughout life's journey, guided by his Spirit and his Gospel. Is it not time that we Christians commit ourselves more seriously to the cause of peacemaking, by doing everything we can to eradicate violence?

Surely the place to start is with ourselves – with our own persons. Destructive violence wears a thousand disguises. Harsh words can be a form of violence, for destruction may be done to another's legitimate self-esteem. Denying a child needed affection is tantamount to violence, for the implicit message is: "You are not worthwhile." To wilfully refuse to visit the elderly, the sick, or the imprisoned, especially when they have a claim on us by blood, is subtly destructive of their personhood; it is to say: "You and your condition are of no particular concern to others." To withhold help from anyone in need, when it is within our capacity to be of assistance, does violence to Christ himself; "Insofar as you neglected to do this to one of the least of these, you neglected to do it to me" (Mt. 25:45).

Once we have struggled to rid violence from our own lives, we will be in a better position to serve as instruments of Christ's peace. Then we can truly contribute to the church's mission of peacemaking by healing the taproots of violence in our neighborhoods, our nation, and our world. For then we will not only have eyes clearly to see those sisters and brothers of ours in the human race who suffer from political, economic and religious oppression. Not only will we be able to commit ourselves, as a united, worldwide community of believers, to assist the human race in retreating from the brink of nuclear holocaust. But we shall have discovered the power for achieving that peace for which all the earth longs: the love of God poured forth on us in abundance on the first Christmas day.

May the song of angels, now almost 2,000 years old, resound for you this Christmas with new meaning and freshness: "To God in the highest, glory; and to all of good will, peace."

Raymond G. Hunthausen,
Archbishop of Seattle

Hunthausen's Christmas letter, 1982

Archbishop Murphy was also known for his pastoral initiatives. He acted on behalf of labor and the rights of workers, he publicly campaigned against certain state initiatives, and supported residents of the timber communities during a time of great need. In 1991 he was outspoken in his attacks against Initiative 119, which would allow doctors to prescribe life-ending medication for terminally ill patients, and Initiative 120, which would re-affirm state abortion rights. In 1993 the archbishop was invited by President Clinton to speak at a national Forest Conference. Archbishop Murphy was often quoted in the op-ed pages of the Seattle *Times* or the *Post Intelligencer*, most notably when he spoke against abortion or against the welfare reform bill proposed by Congress in 1995.

In these and other social welfare concerns, the work of Catholic Charities and Catholic Community Services has expanded significantly since 1975. In 1988, Catholic Community Services of Western Washington (CCSWW) was incorporated as a separate institution, enabling the agency to receive government funding and engage in public-private partnerships. Michael Reichert, President of CCSWW, has led Catholic Charities since 1979, and has helped transform an agency with a $4 million budget and fewer than 200 employees into the largest private non-profit agency providing human and social services in Washington State. CCSWW's annual budget is currently over $60 million and employs over 3,000 people. The archdiocese has also been involved in the expansion of Washington State Catholic Conference (WSCC), an effort on the part of all the bishops in the state to promote Catholic social teachings in the public sphere.

Leadership in ecumenical cooperation has characterized the Archdiocese of Seattle and will continue to mark it well into the new century. Archbishop Hunthausen met regularly with the leaders of other Christian denominations in the region. Locally, ecumenical action was most obvious around issues of social justice, including poverty, racism, and war. Covenants were made with the Episcopal Diocese of

Matt Talbot Center director Greg Alex greeting Murphy, 1995

Prisons and The Christian Conscience

WASHINGTON STATE CATHOLIC CONFERENCE

The Weight To Be Attributed To Teaching In Official Church Documents

Pastoral Statement on the Hispanic People of the State of Washington

Declaración Pastoral Sobre El Pueblo Hispano Del Estado de Washington

Statement on Women

Declaración Sobre La Mujer

A PUBLIC DECLARATION

TO THE TRIBAL COUNCILS AND TRADITIONAL SPIRITUAL LEADERS
OF THE INDIAN AND ESKIMO PEOPLES OF THE PACIFIC NORTHWEST
In care of Jewell Praying Wolf James, Lummi

Seattle, Washington
November 21, 1987

Dear Brothers and Sisters,

This is a formal apology on behalf of our churches for their long-standing participation in the destruction of traditional Native American spiritual practices. We call upon our people for recognition of and respect for your traditional ways of life and for protection of your sacred places and ceremonial objects. We have frequently been unconscious and insensitive and have not come to your aid when you have been victimized by unjust Federal policies and practices. In many other circumstances we reflected the rampant racism and prejudice of the dominant culture with which we too willingly identified. During the 200th Anniversary year of the United States Constitution we, as leaders of our churches in the Pacific Northwest, extend our apology. We ask for your forgiveness and blessing.

As the Creator continues to renew the earth, the plants, the animals and all living things, we call upon the people of our denominations and fellowships to a commitment of mutual support in your efforts to reclaim and protect the legacy of your own traditional spiritual teachings. To that end we pledge our support and assistance in upholding the American Religious Freedom Act (P.L. 95-134, 1978) and within that legal precedent affirm the following:

1) The rights of the Native Peoples to practice and participate in traditional ceremonies and rituals with the same protection offered all religions under the Constitution.
2) Access to and protection of sacred sites and public lands for ceremonial purposes.
3) The use of religious symbols (feathers, tobacco, sweet grass, bones, etc.) for use in traditional ceremonies and rituals.

The spiritual power of the land and the ancient wisdom of your indigenous religions can be, we believe, great gifts to the Christian churches. We offer our commitment to support you in the righting of previous wrongs: To protect your peoples' efforts to enhance Native spiritual teachings; to encourage the members of our churches to stand in solidarity with you on these important religious issues; to provide advocacy and mediation, when appropriate, for ongoing negotiations with State agencies and Federal officials regarding these matters.

May the promises of this day go on public record with all the congregations of our communions and be communicated to the Native American Peoples of the Pacific Northwest. May the God of Abraham and Sarah, and the Spirit who lives in both the cedar and Salmon People be honored and celebrated.

Sincerely,

The Rev. Thomas L. Blevins, Bishop
Pacific Northwest Synod –
Lutheran Church in America

The Most Rev. Raymond G. Hunthausen
Archbishop of Seattle
Roman Catholic Archdiocese of Seattle

The Rev. Dr. Robert Bradford,
Executive Minister
American Baptist Churches of the Northwest

The Rev. Elizabeth Knott, Synod Executive
Presbyterian Church
Synod Alaska-Northwest

The Rev. Robert Brock
N.W. Regional Christian Church

The Rev. Lowell Knutson, Bishop
North Pacific District
American Lutheran Church

The Right Rev. Robert H. Cochrane,
Bishop, Episcopal Diocese of Olympia

The Most Rev. Thomas Murphy
Coadjutor Archbishop
Roman Catholic Archdiocese of Seattle

The Rev. W. James Halfaker
Conference Minister
Washington North Idaho Conference
United Church of Christ

The Rev. Melvin G. Talbert, Bishop
United Methodist Church –
Pacific Northwest Conference

A public declaration to the tribal councils, Nov. 21, 1987

Olympia and with regional Lutheran synods. The archdiocese cooperated in the Church Council of Greater Seattle's apology to Native American peoples that took place in 1987. Archbishop Brunett is a pioneer and architect of the international ecumenical movement and has continued his groundbreaking work in ecumenical and inter-religious affairs in this archdiocese. In addition to bringing his years of insight and expertise to this issue, Archbishop Brunett was appointed in 1999 as the Catholic co-chair of the Anglican-Roman Catholic International Commission (ARCIC) by Pope John Paul II.

The relationship between communities of faith and a bishop has been and continues to be significant to the vitality of a diocese. Archbishop Murphy will always be remembered for his presence at parishes, schools, and faith communities and for his talent to capture an audience with his words and spirit. His ability to travel great distances in an automobile was an inspiration to some and a worry for others, first in the Diocese of Great Falls-Billings, and then in the Archdiocese of Seattle. It is often said that the deepest ruts in the pavement along the I-5 corridor were created by him. Within the first two months of succeeding Archbishop Hunthausen, he set a whirlwind pace of speeches, visits and meetings at parishes and other venues throughout the archdiocese. This pace did not stop for the next six years. Even after he was diagnosed with leukemia in 1996, he continued to be present to the Catholics of the archdiocese. He wrote and spoke about the need to share one's gifts with others unconditionally, especially with the poor. "True compassion," he wrote, "is the willingness to share the pain of others, to be present to them, to learn from them, and to recognize that human life is a gift from God." During the last months of his life, Archbishop Murphy particularly felt the

Archbishop Alex Brunett with George L. Carey, Archbishop of Canterbury (center); John Snyder, Bishop of St. Augustine; and Joseph Gossman, Bishop of Raleigh

importance of sharing this message with the youth of the archdiocese. He died on June 26, 1997 at Providence Hospital in Seattle. He is buried in the crypt in St. James Cathedral.

As Archbishop Alex J. Brunett leads the Archdiocese of Seattle into the 21st century, it is clear that perhaps more than anything else, the archdiocese has awakened to what has been true of it from the beginning: it is a multicultural church. The growth in Hispanic, Asian, and Pacific Islander populations has been significant. Mass and pastoral services continue to be offered in a variety of languages. People across the archdiocese have come to appreciate liturgical celebrations and devotional forms that newer communities have brought with them to the archdiocese. Day of the Dead as it is celebrated by various Hispanic and Latin communities, Kwanzaa for African American/Black Catholics, and *Simbang Gabi* for Filipino Catholics are only a few occasions for celebrating in ways that speak to the holy traditions of God's people.

In recognizing and growing to appreciate its multi-ethnic character, the archdiocese continues

St. Charles Church, Burlington

Kwanzaa prayer service, John Nwanze, St. John Bosco Church, Tacoma

Gudelia Alejo, Day of the Dead altar, St. Mary Church, Seattle

Simbang Gabi procession

St. Joseph Church, Vancouver

to help Catholic immigrants, recent and distant, adjust to their new social and cultural context while retaining and being nourished by their faith. Archbishop Brunett has responded to the particular formation and leadership needs of these communities by allocating resources toward training and educating key sacramental, educational, and pastoral ministers for parishes and faith communities throughout the archdiocese. New directions are being forged. As the Catholic Church of the Archdiocese of Seattle experiences growing numbers, an active laity, and renewed life in Catholic schools and religious education, it faces the challenges of providing effective pastoral ministry to a culturally and demographically diverse Catholic population. Adults have grown in spirituality and have assumed the mantle of responsibility through change, while the youth demand truth. The church is its people and its shared history is the collection of their words and deeds. The signs of vitality, commitment, and openness to the spirit are apparent. The Archdiocese of Seattle is indeed blessed with an abundance of grace.

Blessed Sacrament Church, Seattle

Archbishop Alex J. Brunett, Palm Sunday

Immaculate Conception Church, Seattle

Archbishop Brunett (c) saying Mass at Lummi Reservation

Pastoral statement on inclusion

OPEN WIDE THE DOORS TO CHRIST

PASTORAL STATEMENT

BY

ARCHBISHOP ALEX J. BRUNETT

November 16, 1998

Archbishop Brunett arrives at Tulalip reservation, Aug. 28, 1999

BIBLIOGRAPHY

- Archives of the Archdiocese of Seattle and the Catholic Schools Department. *Pride in Our Past/Faith in Our Future: Catholic Northwest History Curriculum.* Seattle: Archdiocese of Seattle, 1999.
- Archives of the Archdiocese of Seattle. Records. Biographical, Bishops, *Catholic Northwest Progress,* Correspondence, Education, Parishes, Organizations.
- Blanchet, Bishop Augustin Magloire. *Letter Books.* Archives, Archdiocese of Seattle.
- Blanchet, Francis Norbert, Archbishop. *Historical Sketches of the Catholic Church in Oregon and the Northwest.* Ferndale, WA: 1910.
- Buerge, David M. and Junius Rochester. *Roots and Branches: The Religious Heritage of Washington State.* Seattle: Church Council of Greater Seattle, 1988.
- Burns, Jeffrey M. "Building the Best: A History of Catholic Parish Life in the Pacific States." In Jay P. Dolan, ed. *The American Catholic Parish; A History from 1850 to the Present.* New York: Paulist Press, 1987.
- Burns, Robert I., S.J. *The Jesuits and Indian Wars of the Northwest.* New Haven: Yale University Press, 1966.
- Carey, Patrick W. *The Roman Catholics in America.* Westport, CT: Praeger, 1996.
- Carriker, Robert C. *Father Peter John De Smet: Jesuit in the West.* Norman: University of Oklahoma Press, 1995.
- *Catholic Northwest Progress.* 1900-2000. Special topical supplements, 1969-1987.
- *Catholic Northwest Progress, 75th Anniversary.* Vol. 75, no. 42, October 20, 1972.
- *Centennial of the Archdiocese of Seattle (1850-1950).* Seattle: Northwest Progress, 1950.
- Clark, Norman H. *The Dry Years: Prohibition and Social Change in Washington.* Revised Edition. Seattle: University of Washington Press, 1988.
- Clark, Norman H. *Washington: a Bicentennial History.* New York: Norton, 1976.
- Cordova, Fred, ed. *Filipinos! Forgotten Asian Americans.* Dubuque: Kendall Hunt, 1983.
- Cronin, Kay. *Cross in the Wilderness.* Mitchell Press, 1960.
- Crowley, Walt. *Seattle University: A Century of Jesuit Education.* Seattle: Seattle University, 1991.
- Davis, Cyprian. *The History of Black Catholics in the United States.* New York: Crossroad, 1990.
- Dolan, Jay P. *The American Catholic Experience: A History from Colonial Times to the Present.* New York: Doubleday, 1985.
- Doogan, Monsignor John P. "From Log Cabin to Cathedral." Unpublished manuscript in the Archives of the Archdiocese of Seattle.
- Duncan, Janice K. *Minority without a Champion: Kanakas on the Pacific Coast, 1788-1850.* Portland: Oregon Historical Society, 1972.
- Duntley, Madeline. "Japanese and Filipino Together: The Transethnic Vision of Our Lady Queen of Martyrs Parish." *U.S. Catholic Historian* 18/1 (Winter 2000): 74-98.
- Gibson, James R. *The Lifeline of the Oregon Country: The Fraser-Columbia Brigade System, 1811-1847.* Vancouver: University of British Columbia Press, 1997.
- Haeberlin, Hermann and Erna Gunther. *The Indians of Puget Sound.* Seattle: University of Washington Press, 1973.
- Hennessy, James. *American Catholics: A History of the Roman Catholic Community in the United States.* New York: Oxford University Press, 1981.
- "Histories/Handbook of Pastoral Practices." Draft Manuscript, Asian Pacific American Affairs Desk, Archdiocese of Seattle.
- Johansen, Bruce E. and Roberto F. Maestas. *The Creation of Washington's Latino Community: 1935-1980.* Seattle: El Centro de la Raza, 1981.

■ Keller-Scholz, Rick. "The Other Nisqually Missions: Catholic Missionaries and the Hudson's Bay Company in the Pacific Northwest." *Occurrences: The Journal of Northwest History During the Fur Trade*, 17, no. 3 (Summer 1999): 3-8.

■ Killen, Patricia O'Connell and Christine Taylor. "Washington State." in *The Encyclopedia of the Irish in America.* Edited by Michael Glazier. South Bend: University of Notre Dame Press, 1999.

■ Kowrach, Edward J., ed. *Journal of a Catholic Bishop on the Oregon Trail: The Overland Crossing of the Rt. Rev. A.M.A. Blanchet, Bishop of Walla Walla, from Montreal to Oregon Territory, March 23, 1847 to January 23, 1851.* Fairfield, WA: Ye Galleon Press, 1978.

■ Landholm, Cark, ed. *Notes and Voyages of the Famed Quebec Missions to the Pacific Northwest.* Portland: Oregon Historical Society, Champoeg Press, Reed College, 1956.

■ Lucia, Ellis. *Seattle's Sisters of Providence: The Story of Providence Medical Center, Seattle's First Hospital.* Seattle: Sisters of Providence, 1978.

■ McCrosson, Sister Mary of the Blessed Sacrament. *The Bell and the River.* Palo Alto, CA: Pacific Books, 1957.

■ Metz, William J., Fr. "History of the Catholic Church in the State of Washington." Unpublished Manuscript, Archives of the Archdiocese of Seattle.

■ Metz, William J., Fr. "Diocese of Seattle." *Catholic Encylopedia,* Vol. 13. New York: Robert Appleton Company, 1912: 665-667.

■ Munnick, Harriet Duncan and Mikell de Lores Wormell Warner. *Catholic Church Records of the Pacific Northwest: Vancouver Volumes I & II and Stellamaris Missions.* Vancouver, WA: French Prairie Press, 1972.

■ O'Connell, William P. "Fifty Golden Years." The *Catholic Northwest Progress,* November 1932.

■ O'Hara, Edwin V. *Pioneer Catholic History of Oregon.* Centennial Edition. Paterson, NJ: St. Anthony Guild Press, 1939.

■ Ruby, Robert H. and John A. Brown. *A Guide to the Indian Tribes of the Pacific Northwest.* Norman: University of Oklahoma Press, 1992.

■ Schoenberg, Wilfred P., S.J. *Gonzaga University: Seventy-Five Years, 1887-1962.* Spokane: Gonzaga University, 1963.

■ Schoenberg, Wilfred P., S.J. *A History of the Catholic Church in the Pacific Northwest, 1743-1983.* Washington, D.C.: The Pastoral Press, 1987.

■ Schwantes, Carlos Arnaldo. *The Pacific Northwest: An Interpretive History.* Revised and Enlarged Edition. Lincoln: University of Nebraska Press, 1996.

■ Scott, James W. and Roland L. De Lorme. *Historical Atlas of Washington.* Norman: University of Oklahoma Press, 1988.

■ Scott, John C., O.S.B. *This Place Called Saint Martin's, 1895-1995: A Centennial History of Saint Martin's College and Abbey, Lacey, Washington.* Donning Company, 1996.

■ Seling, Mary. *St. Vincent De Paul in Seattle, 75 Years.* Seattle: Unique Press, 1995.

■ Takami, David A. *Divided Destiny: A History of Japanese Americans in Seattle.* Seattle, WA: University of Washington Press, 1998.

■ Taylor, Quintard. *In Search of the Racial Frontier: African Americans in the American West, 1528-1990.* New York: W.W. Norton, 1998.

■ Taylor, Quintard. *The Forging of a Black Community: Seattle's Central District from 1870 through the Civil Rights Era.* Seattle: University of Washington Press, 1994.

■ Treacy, Fr. William. *Love Bears All Things: Bridging Troubled Waters.* Seattle: Peanut Butter Press, 1994.

■ Twohy, Patrick J., S.J. *Finding a Way Home: Indian and Catholic Spiritual Paths of the Plateau Tribes.* Spokane: Gonzaga University Press, 1983.

■ White, Sid and S.E. Solberg, eds. *Peoples of Washington: Perspectives on Cultural Diversity.* Pullman, WA: Washington State University Press, 1989.